Hire by Design

A Hiring Blueprint with Design Thinking

Jodi Brandstetter

PUBLISHING

"Straightforward and accessible, this book provides actionable recommendations companies can action now to improve their hiring processes by making it more human-focused."

Frida Polli PhD, CEO and co-founder, pymetrics.

"This will become your playbook for talent acquisition! *Hire by Design* isn't a book you will read once and put on a shelf. It's a book you will pick up again and again. It is filled with practical strategies that are easily understood and will become the playbook for your talent acquisition strategy. Using real life examples, Brandstetter weaves a story applicable to every company no matter size, industry, or structure."

Nick Dokich, CEO, ULIMI

"Finally - a real playbook for the TA space! Jodi breaks recruiting strategy down for hiring teams of all sizes in a practical way. She expertly scrapes away the philosophical "fluff" and provides tactical advice that you can implement immediately. With loads of case studies and tangible examples, she walks you through the "why" behind each approach. *Hire by Design* will literally coach you through nearly any recruiting scenario and arm you with the knowledge you need to forge a strategic path forward to hit your hiring goals."

Kelley J. Cox, Talent Acquisition Leader, Amazon

"Effective Recruiting and Talent Acquisition professionals are a critical component of any company's success because understanding how to attract and recruit the talent that is needed will determine whether they will be successful with executing the organization's strategic objectives. Unfortunately, there are few books that provide helpful guidance to recruiting and TA pros in understanding the foundations and strategies necessary to do their jobs well. This book is a great resource for anyone looking to grow in their skills, which will ultimately help their organizations to grow as well."

Jennifer McClure - CEO of Unbridled Talent LLC and Chief Excitement Officer of DisruptHR LLC

"*Hire by Design* is the perfect engine for driving Talent Acquisition to a new level. Our times demand change and we are fortunate to have the tools available through Hire by Design to craft a new path forward."

Gerry Crispin, Principal & Co-founder, CareerXroads

"We keep thinking 'Talent' is a mix of skills and attributes only. Jodi shows us that 'Talent' is so much more. By implementing a design thinking approach, we identify and bring a human-centric lens to having great humans join our organizations. This book gives you a tangible roadmap to be intentional and effective in doing this well."

Steve Browne, SHRM-SCP, VP of Human Resources, LaRosa's, Inc. and Author of *HR on Purpose!!* and *HR Rising!!*

"I've been a fan of the use of Design Thinking in Recruiting for years and Jodi has written the perfect guide for how TA and HR leaders can easily bring this strategy into their own organizations. Turns out, design or lack thereof, is a major factor in why candidates either choose you or don't choose you!"

Tim Sackett, Author of *The Talent Fix* and CEO of HRUTech.com

This book is dedicated to my daughter, Lena Marcella. Your name may be from our family history, but you are our future. What I do is for you. Love you back!

CONTENTS

TEMPLATES

ACKNOWLEDGMENTS

When writing a book, it takes a tribe. I want to thank everyone who helped me onthis journey. You all gave me the confidence to take the leap and provided lots of feedback and support.

Adriana Monique Alvarez – my book coach and mentor – Thank you for reaching out to me and asking to connect. Our conversation confirmed that I can and will write a book! You have been amazing!

Dylan Gadzala – PR Intern and Editor – Thank you for supporting me by providing the first edit of the book. I see great things for you in your future!

Dot Miller – Editor – Thank you for taking time to provide edits and your creativity for the book. You have been a mentor to me and I appreciate all that you did!

Frida Polli, PhD – Thank you for taking the time to speak to me about pymetrics and to provide your thoughts on talent acquisition and technology.

Gerry Crispin – Thank you for taking the time to read and provide a testimonial. It is an honor to be in the same industry.

Tim Sackett – Thank you for reading and providing a testimonial. Your book inspired me to write my book. Virtual hug!

Steve Browne – Thank you for taking the time to read and provide a testimonial. Your book also inspired me and your love for HR is compelling.

Nick Dokich – Thank you for taking the time to read and provide a testimonial. I have enjoyed working with you and the ULIMI team.

Jennifer McClure - Thank you for taking the time to read and provide a testimonial. You have been an influencer and a supporter to me and so many others.

Kelley Cox – Thank you for being a great friend and providing a testimonial. Your support and love mean so much.

Talent Acquisition Evolution Community – Thank you for being a community where we can network, learn, laugh, and work together.

Talent Acquisition Mastermind Group – Thank you for the support and encouragement while writing.

Larry and Becky Harmeyer – best parents – Thank you for teaching me that I can do anything with hard work, integrity, and positivity. Your love has helped me grow to be the best person and mom that I can be. Love you!

Ron Brandstetter – my amazing husband and best friend – You are my buddy, my pal, my love, and my everything. Thank you for supporting me through all my crazy ideas from starting a business to writing this book. I love you.

Lena Brandstetter – my sweet child – When you came into this world, I understood unconditional love. Everything I do I think of you. I am a better person because of you. I am excited to see where you go in life, and I will cheer you on as much as you cheer me on. Love you back.

Dali and Monet Brandstetter – my sweet fur children – Thank you for the unconditional love and companionship at home (especially during shelter in place!).

Thank you to my family, friends, and network who have provided love, support and feedback through the years.

INTRODUCTION

Being a Recruiter, I never thought that I would write a book. I was more likely to recruit a writer. But if you asked me what type of book I wanted write, I would say a book on talent acquisition.

From the very beginning, I loved everything about talent acquisition, from talking to people about their career to the excitement for someone who accepts a new job. This passion started in college when I completed an internship in Human Resources at a hospital. My job was to recruit Patient Care Assistants, and this experience made me realize the impact that hiring had on the care of patients. After that, I wanted to have a career in human resources and, especially, in recruiting.

Throughout my career, my focus was talent acquisition—from hiring temps for companies in downtown Cincinnati, collectors for a financial services company, inside sales for a logistics company, to information technology professional for banks and healthcare. And, each company and each hire gave me the ability to understand the selection and hiring process and best practices in talent acquisition.

My last corporate role was a Director of Talent Acquisition where I had a team of recruiters throughout the country that hired call center professionals. This role gave me the ability to focus on training and managing recruiters and creating a streamline user-friendly selection process. I knew that I wanted to be able to work with more companies to ensure their process was streamline and effective, and their talent acquisition team had the tools and skills to be successful at hiring the best talent for their company.

After being in the corporate world for 16 years, I decided to start my own consulting business that focused on creating talent acquisition processes that helped companies become an Employer of Choice. While networking with job seekers and leaders in different businesses, I noticed that there were several areas in the selection process and the talent acquisition strategy that needed to be re-vamped or updated.

While building my business, I wanted to find a methodology that could help build the best talent acquisition strategies, selection and hiring processes, and people experiences. After learning about design thinking, I fell in love with the methodology and knew this would be the best methodology to build strong talent acquisition strategies, processes, and experiences. Design thinking focused on the needs and desires of people and ensured that the solution was feasible and viable for a business. The method evolved over the years; and, now, throughout this book, I will focus on how I use my design thinking method with my clients.

When I was researching and learning about design thinking, I came across IDEO U which is the arm of IDEO, a global design company, that provides courses and certifications in design thinking. I completed both their Foundations in Design Thinking Certification and the Advance Design Thinking Certification. To find out more about this program, please go to *www. ideaou.com.*

is book takes the reader through the different steps of design thinking with a talent acquisition focus. Also, at the end of the book and through *www.HireByDesignBook.com,* there are templates to help with the different steps of design thinking and the selection process. I encourage you to try out each step along the way. Learn through practice.

By purchasing this book, I know that you are also someone committed to improving the selection and hiring process. And for that I thank you!

## ONE

A PERSPECTIVE ON TALENT ACQUISITION AND DESIGN THINKING

Introduction

Professionals in the business world have always examined the need for qualified workers and worker shortage; however, the terminologies and methods have continually changed. Since the dynamics of work will continue to evolve, companies must change their procedures as well. Currently, companies are struggling to find the right talent. For example, the Conference Board Survey states that attracting and retaining talent is the top internal concern for chief executives in 2020.[1] For small businesses, iHire's 2019 survey states that 64.2% of small businesses are struggling to attract qualified talent.[2] To meet the changing need, companies look for state of the art technology to incorporate or refinement of their selection process to improve their ability to find talent.

Talent Acquisition

Talent Acquisition, the timely term for recruiting qualified candidates, has evolved over the past 20+ years. Companies have gone from using mail and fax to using email and job boards and have recently evolved to bots and texts. Just like other service focused areas, hiring has gone digital and automated. Now, even a Robot can conduct a face to face interview. Therefore, any company hiring, now and in the future, will need to adopt new strategies, including new approaches, technologies, and processes. Companies do not have the luxury of time to sift through tons of unqualified resumes or have candidates jump through hoops to get the job. Companies need to focus on streamlining efficient processes that focus on the candidate experience while showcasing their company brand, work environment, and core values.

In the same Conference Board Survey, the number one external factor that concerns chief executives is a recession.[3] In the Global Business Outlook CFO survey (April 2019), the author states that 67% of US CFOs believe that the US will be in recession by the third quarter of 2020.[4]

Currently, April 2020, people are sheltering in place due to a COVID 19 pandemic, and almost 17 million Americas have filed for unemployment. Some economists say that unemployment will exceed the twenty-five percent peak during the Great Depression.[5] Also, as in the Great Recession of 2007, some companies are on a hiring freeze while others like healthcare, supply chains and grocery industries have increased their hiring during this pandemic.

Findings from the 2007 recession has provided companies with information for survival, recovery, and continued success on how to survive during, recover after, and thrive through a major threat. A *Harvard Business Review* study reports that 17% of companies in the survey did not survive and that only 9% of their sample thrived.[6] One wonders: "What strategies help companies thrive?" The *HBR* article also states, "The companies most likely to outperform their competitors after a recession are pragmatic. The CEOs of pragmatic companies recognize that cost cutting is necessary to survive a recession, that investment is equally essential to spur growth..."[7] One way this can be achieved is to cut costs by improving operational efficiency and by developing new business opportunities. Another example is to cut staff to lower cost, which, in turn, presents another problem when the need for hiring expands. It is also common for costs to increase and for performance to plummet.

Momentum is lost when hiring stops. Hiring is not a button one can push and have people lining up at the door. The best idea is to continue to hire roles that are needed during this time and focus on maintaining a strong employer brand. When hiring lessens, the company leaders can step back and review the current processes, resources, and policies to see if they need to be updated or enhanced.

As the economy changes, it is easy to note that hiring often follows suit. It can feel like a roller coaster when the company goes from a hiring blitz to a hiring freeze. It can also feel like a hamster wheel, where one is just consistently doing the same thing repeatedly. What is certain, however, is that companies need people; and not just anyone either but the right person for the job. To find that right person, the right talent acquisition strategy must be in place.

When investing in a strong talent acquisition strategy, companies will see a return on investment. One of these strong strategies is design thinking, a methodology that will focus on the right people by understanding who they are and where to find them. By having a targeted approach, companies will potentially save time, cut hiring costs, and increase productivity in all areas of the business.

Integration of Design Thinking into Talent Acquisition

Using design thinking to create ideas in hiring is not a new idea. Companies are currently using it and even incorporating new technology in the design. One example (provided below) is the partnership of IDEO, a global design company, with American Family Insurance.

American Family once asked IDEO to come up with an idea to help working families who needed a financial cushion for any possible emergencies or for an unexpected event. American Family's idea was a budgeting tool. By using design thinking, IDEO realized that the families first needed a way to get enough to save. IDEO interviewed and observed families in all different places. It turned out that everyone knew how to budget but did not have enough money and did not want to add more debt. What they wanted was extra work to make more money.

IDEO then asked the question, "Could we offer people who already have jobs the extra hours and income they need in a way that reduces, rather than exacerbates, the stress they already face? Would employers get on board?" The answer was yes.

Also, since many companies rely on seasonal and temporary staff for on-demand work, IDEO presented the idea of creating a service to help families bridge the money gap by finding short term work. This resulted in a business venture called Moonrise. Its platform lets people sign up for shifts posted by partner companies, and the people who work for them are considered Moonrise employees. As such, the hires do not have to pay self-employment taxes, which can be a buffer or can help someone try out a new field or industry.

IDEO and American Family conducted a real time test of Moonrise by getting 11 "Moonrisers," six employers, and a design and programming team to work out any issues with the platform. During the week-long live test, Moonrisers finished a combined 28 work shifts, earning an average of $121 each; and the design and programming team was able to ensure the platform ran smoothly.

American Family then decided to create a startup company called Moonrise and launched it to the public in the Chicago area in 2018 where it would eventually go nationwide. Since Moonrise started in 2018, they have paid over $500,000 to Moonrisers. They also expanded into three additional states in 2019.

Using design thinking, the result of the study was that what American Family "thought" their customers needed was not what they "actually" needed. The design thinking approach allowed customer's needs to emerge and then identified the most appropriate solution for them.[8]

Since design thinking focuses on the needs and desires of people and ensures that the solution is feasible and viable for a business, it is a "no brainer" to come up with the best talent acquisition strategies, resources, processes, and experience for both the business and the candidates. Companies need to stay on top of their talent acquisition strategy no matter the state of the economy so that they can push forward and continue their business success.

At first glance, it's easy to wonder: "What is design thinking?" and "How can you really use it to create ideas and solutions for hiring?" These and other questions will be discussed in the next chapter.

TWO
DESIGN THINKING

Introduction

Organizations use design thinking to create innovative ideas for all phases of their operations. IDEO is a global design company that has used design thinking in the process of developing innovative human-focused products, services, technology, and experiences. An anecdote of one of their real-world challenges may provide an understanding of design thinking.

IDEO, along with the creative agency called Forpeople, assisted Intercontinental Hotels Group (IHG) with defining and launching a new brand focused on short-stay travelers for their industry. IHG's goal was to exceed the expectations of those travelers while balancing quality and price. As a result, the group generated the following question: "What kind of offer might resonate equally with guests and with owners/operators who would need to buy into a new brand and bring it to life?"

IDEO began by talking to people who typically only traveled a few times a year, took short trips to smaller cities, or lived on the road by moving from hotel to hotel. Based on this research, IDEO created two prototypes for

IHG. IHG brought potential customers and hotel owners together to discuss the two prototypes and to get feedback on the new format and experience.

The feedback about the prototypes provided helpful insights. The main concern for potential customers was the quality of the hotel, including its safety, cleanliness, and ability to get a good night's sleep. Also, the discussion revealed that these customers were not interested in any fancy or extravagant services, including communication. Given this feedback, IDEO was convinced the selected brand would alleviate the concerns and ultimately reward the guest with the desired cleanliness, comfy mattress, grab and go breakfast, and friendly atmosphere with straightforward communication.

As a result of the above design thinking process, IHG created Avid™ hotels that were designed to deliver quality services with a sense of focus and afford-ability. Within a year of partnering with IDEO, IHG had issued 150 Avid™ hotel licenses in the US, Mexico, and Canada.[1]

What is design thinking?

When most people encounter the term "design thinking," they envision creating a new product or a tangible item; however, design thinking is so much more. Design thinking focuses on a human-centered approach to generating innovative ideas and solutions.

Tim Brown, Executive Chair of IDEO gives this as the definition of design thinking:

Design thinking is a human-centered approach to innovation that draws from the designer's toolkit to integrate the needs of people, the possibilities of technology, and the requirements for business success.[2]

When using design thinking, the leader of the design thinking experience focuses 100% on the whole person– their skills, talents, emotions, or drives —whether it be the customer, client, candidate, and so on. To do this, it is imperative to hear directly from the clients rather than providing them with information they repeat as their response. The approach of each client is unique, and the process must adjust to his/her perspective.

The design thinking process requires taking a problem and approaching it with design thinking-based tools like brainstorming, storyboards, and ideologies focused on empathy and gathering insights. The process focuses on what the participants desire, while at the same time making sure the solution is viable and within given limits. In essence, design thinking requires viewing the problem through three lenses: desirability, feasibility and viability.

Lenses	Definition
Desirability	Understanding people's dreams, wants, and desires to propose a solution that addresses what they need and value.
Feasibility	Having practicability, and achievability.
Viability	Making business sense and sustainable.

3

In design thinking, following the three lenses will ensure the solution meets the criteria for success for the user and the business. IDEO U is an online school created to teach the IDEO methods to help individuals, teams, and organizations across the globe become more resilient, creative, and innovative. IDEO U's design thinking strategy has nine steps. Working through these nine steps will provide a framework to define the challenge by gathering insights and creating prototypes.[4]

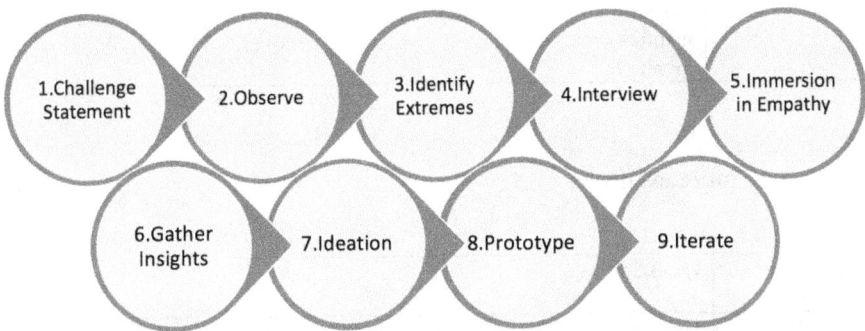

1.Challenge Statement   2.Observe   3.Identify Extremes   4.Interview   5.Immersion in Empathy   6.Gather Insights   7.Ideation   8.Prototype   9.Iterate

Challenge Statement

The first step in the design thinking process is having a question that needs answering. Typically, the question starts like this: How might we …? Given the question, a picture of what is currently happening and the need for a new solution emerges. This image will determine the Challenge Statement.

Using the imagery of *Goldilocks and the Three Bears*, three types of questions emerge: Is it too broad and unmanageable, too narrow and limits the possible solutions, or is it Goldilocks's "just right" which is focused on need, broad enough to make discoveries, and manageable. The table below gives examples of each type of question.

Type of Example	Question	Response
Too Broad	How might we create a space that inspires creativity?	This is too broad because there is no focus and it is not manageable. Different departments, locations, and forms of leadership can also make this too broad.
Too Narrow	How might we create a working environment in our marketing department at headquarters that inspires creativity which in turns creates loyalty?	That is too small because again there is no focus on need and no room to discover. The focus is only on a minute detail of the problem, and it is way too specific.
Just Right	How might we create a working environment that inspires creativity and loyalty?	This is "just right" because it focuses on a need, it is manageable, and there is room to discover.

Here is one more example:

Type of Example	Question
Too Big	How might we help our leaders understand unconscious bias?
Too Narrow	How might we encourage our leaders to complete an unconscious bias training?
Just Right	How might we encourage our leaders to learn more about unconscious bias and take these learnings to their teams?

To ensure that the questions work, however, the following clarifying questions may be asked:

1. Is the solution included in the problem statement? If so, there is no room for creative ideas.
2. Is the question inspiring enough to motivate someone to solve the challenge?
3. Is the audience narrow enough? Will the question generate the requisite needs and concerns?
4. Is there a specific time or moment given for the design?
5. Is the question interesting?

Using the first "Just Right" example—How might we create a working environment that inspires creativity and loyalty?—and looking at the five questions above, the original question can be tweaked to be more focused, inspiring, time specific, and interesting. It might become "How might we create an onboarding experience (the first couple of weeks of employment) for our new hires that will inspire loyalty and dedication to our core values and ensure that the hires are inspired to create their best work?" Using this question, the issue becomes focused on one specific moment "onboarding;" a specific audience, namely the new hires; and more texture.

Observation

Once the challenge statement is generated, the second step in design thinking is observing. Companies typically rely on focus groups to ask questions and engage their employees or customers on specific items like a new product idea or change in policy, etc. However, observing the person in action is more effective because it provides better insights into whether he/she follows the process or has any work arounds, i.e., strategies to alleviate problems that arise. Following is a personal example of the importance of observation in design thinking.

While working at an IT Staffing Firm, I was observing one of my co-workers conducting a technical interview. My co-worker had index cards with questions specific to the skill. It helped ensure that she asked the right questions during the conversation. It was a great idea to make sure that we as a team asked the same questions. But why index cards? Was that the best way to gather that information? As a team, we decided that we needed a place in our Applicant Tracking System (ATS) where we could select a skill set and have specific questions appear depending on what skill sets were selected. Using this process was a more effective way of handling the questioning in an interview. Since I was an administrator for the ATS, I was able to employ this system. Without observation of this teammate, I would have never known the questioning process needed refining.

Such observation requires planning. Who is the person designated to be observed? Where are they located—online or in person? What is the reason for the observation? What is going to spark the observer's curiosity? What type of themes is the observer looking for? Observation also requires listening with the eyes. It does not mean asking questions—that is an interview. Observation requires being open and nonjudgmental. The observer must focus on what, how, and why. What are they doing? How are they doing it? Why are they doing it? Are there any "prompt" behaviors, "workarounds," adaptations, patterns, or anything unexpected they are doing to create a better or easier process?

Taking notes is crucial. Notes must be taken about the environment, resources, and the interactions being exhibited. The notes should again address the who, what, and why questions. Cameras may be used for authenticity and future use.

After observing a few people, notes are reviewed and critical observations recorded. The observer must write down at least three observations that were of special interest, peaked curiosity, and that noted the motivation for the behavior observed. This information will help generate the questions for the interview step.

Identify Extremes

When looking for a solution that is human focused, the interviewer must understand the audience, including the extremes and the mainstream. The extreme audience is a group of people who either have no experience or a lot of experience, whereas the mainstream is having the average amount of experience. The range of an audience can look like a bell-shaped curve. The extremes are at both ends and the mainstream is in the middle where the curve is the highest.

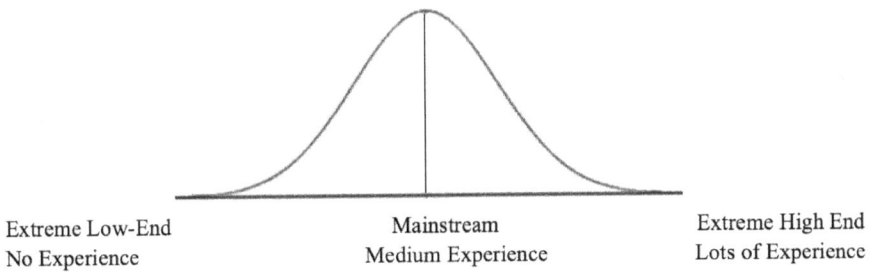

Extreme Low-End	Mainstream	Extreme High End
No Experience	Medium Experience	Lots of Experience

Typically, an individual only considers the middle or mainstream of the spectrum when coming up with ideas. It is important to also include the extremes on both sides of the spectrum. If an idea works for one of the extremes, it will typically work for the mainstream as well. When talking to persons at the extremes, their unique creativity begins flowing and ideas emerge that may generate the ideal solution to a situation.

How do you identify extremes? There are varied ways of identifying the extremes: demographics, behaviors, and motivations. From there, the imagination stretches to the very edges of the spectrum. Such a stretch within the interviewing situation will look something like this:

Stretch = Level of Interviewing Experience

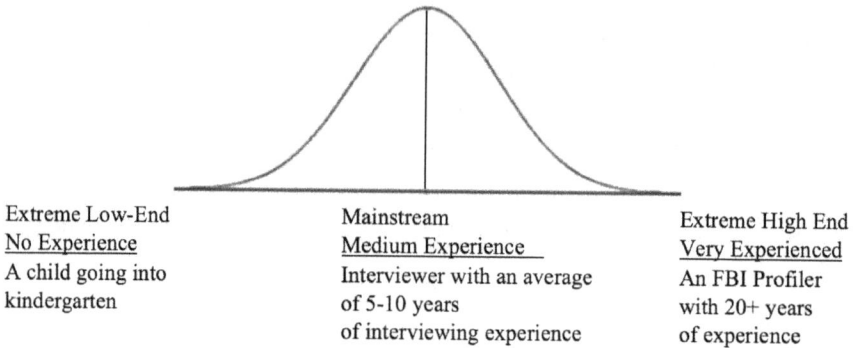

Extreme Low-End	Mainstream	Extreme High End
No Experience	Medium Experience	Very Experienced
A child going into kindergarten	Interviewer with an average of 5-10 years of interviewing experience	An FBI Profiler with 20+ years of experience

Given these two extreme groups, a picture emerges of different people who fit into those extremes. These pictures can be built from the profile of the demographics plus observed behaviors of the following:

- Level of expertise
- Attitudes
- Familiarity with product/service
- Technology/social media

With this information, the individual is selected who will provide an extreme perspective. Moreover, the information from the profile and observed behaviors will facilitate developing questions for the interview.

Interviewing

Conducting a productive interview helps provide the best information to move forward with the challenge statement. A great interview involves two major steps: (1) select the individuals to interview, while making sure to include someone from the extremes and (2) identify the topics to explore and create about ten questions. The questions should range from getting to know the person to specific questions for the challenge statement, as well as a few that focus on the extreme attitudes or behaviors.

Interview questions should be open ended questions, such as "Can you show me…?" or "Tell me about a time when…." There should not be any Yes or

No questions. Also, it is important to probe after they answer a question. To do this, the interviewer asks questions, such as "Why?" or "Can you tell me more?" Digging deep will provide a more complete picture of the interviewee. The interviewer should feel free to ask questions that may sound naïve, but they should not get distracted with irrelevant questions. People do like to explain their logic or how they came up with something, so allow some flexibility. It can be uncomfortable when the person pauses or does not start talking after the question is asked. Pauses are fine, and the person should have time to think about the questions. The interviewer should not force their thoughts on the client. When they are ready, they will answer the question. It is important to stay unbiased and nonjudgmental during this interview.

Before beginning, expectations for the interview need to be established and explained to the interviewee: the length of the interview, the reason for the information requested, and an explanation of how the meeting is being recorded (taking notes, or using voice/video recording) and why. Generally, interviews begin with introductions. The interviewer introduces himself/herself and encourages the interviewee to share information as well. A discussion of the project follows and, hopefully, the interchange of information and ideas results in building rapport. The interviewer can use multiple strategies to build rapport. Body language shows clients that they are important and are being heard. Another strategy is to lean forward, which gives the appearance of being interested and engaged. Also, expressions, such as smiling and nodding, show active listening. Of primary importance is that the interviewer is primarily listening, and the interviewee is doing most of the talking.

If taking notes or watching the interview, the interviewer writes any interesting quotes, problems, opportunities, ideas, and insights from the interview. Also, photos of the person, the location of the interview, or any object being discussed in the interview are also helpful.

After conducting the interviews, the next step is reflection on the notes and information collected. Were there any common themes? Any extremes that came through? Any insights that need to be built upon?

Immersion in Empathy

Having gathered insights about the candidate, the interviewer can now focus on empathy. To immerse in empathy is to put oneself in the other person's shoes. How are their perspectives and actions different? Here is a personal example of when I used immersion in empathy.

As a talent acquisition professional, I am immersed into the hiring process from the business perspective. There are times when I do not see the other side of the hiring process—the candidate experience. In order to immerse in empathy, I had to talk to job seekers to get the candidate experience.

While conducting a case study on communication, I sat down with job seekers to understand their experiences. We discussed the different communications they received throughout the hiring process and they explained to me what kind of communication they wanted and why.

What I learned from this experience was that job seekers want to get a heads up on where they are in the process even if there is no news to provide. Just a quick note that says, "You are still in the process. Nothing to report right now." This gives them a moment of clarity about whether they are still being considered or not. Most of the job seekers were ok with the process being long if they knew where they stood in the process.

I was focused on communications about the next step or end of the interview process, and I was not thinking about the times when there is nothing to report and how that can provide anxiety or uncertainty to the job seeker.

There are four ways to create an immersive empathy experience.

1. Change your perspective – Think of ways to change your perspective to relate to someone who sees things differently. This is the experience used in the example above.
2. Limit Yourself – Take an ability away and explore that experience.

For example, if the person utilizes the bus to work, how will that possibly impact them on what work schedule he/she can do?

3. Do It Yourself – Try out the product, service, or experience firsthand. For example, apply to the career site and see what a candidate experiences.

4. Engage in an Analogous Experience – Experience yourself what you are designing analogously. Here is an example. Bots are one way to communicate to your candidate pool via your website. Being able to see how a bot handles questions from a different industry (Banking, Retail, etc.) clarifies what a candidate wants from a bot on a career page.[5]

To use empathy, the interviewer comes up with five different questions to answer. The question starts with "What does it feel like to …?" From these questions, create 8-10 experiences using the "immersive empathy" criteria above to get a new or different perspective. Then, select one to practice and learn. Again, reflection on any new insights observed provides for a more enriching immersion into empathy experience.

Gather Insights

The whole reason a person observes, interacts with extremes, interviews, and immerses in empathy is to find insights into how to move forward in finding a solution or idea for the challenge statement. Part of the process is to pull all the notes from each section and connect them together through themes or patterns. Once some themes or patterns emerge, the next steps are to review the notes again and create new insights. The insights should be informed, inspired, and memorable. Having built insights, the person needs to get feedback from the stakeholders. Also, they can tell stories from their insights to others and gain feedback that way, or they can create a quick presentation. Once confident with the insights, it is time to summarize via storytelling.

Storytelling is sharing ideas in story form with others. It can be through photography, video, or even puppets! When sharing the story, be specific and provide actual stories, paint the picture through words or actual pictures, be descriptive, and make sure the work is correctly presented. Using storyboards is highly effective—and entertaining—especially when focusing on a service or experience-based problem.

Ideation

Once all the above steps have been completed, it is now time to take the insights generated and come up with ideas to solve the challenge statement. This is the fun part – Ideation. Ideation is the process of creating ideas from the insights gathered. Ideation is all about ideas and coming up with them quickly. This process gives a person the ability to look at several different ways to solve the problem. When people ideate, they have to bring their creativity and open mind. No decisions are made during ideation. This is all about coming up with lots of possible ideas.

There are four different Ideation Methods:

1. Brainstorm – get a group together and let the ideas flow.
2. Mash Up – take two completely different things and put them together to generate creative or original ideas.
3. Other People's Shoe-Storm –look at different perspectives in order to come up with new ideas.
4. E-storming – get ideas from individuals who are not in the office using electronic devices.[6]

Once the ideation session is completed, the group needs to review the ideas and put similar ideas into piles or clusters. At this point, themes will start to emerge. After discussing each theme, have the group vote for their top three to five ideas. The ideas with the most votes will be the ideas used to discuss potential prototypes and, ultimately, the chosen idea.

Prototype

Haven chosen the idea; the group is ready to build its prototype. There are several different ways to create a prototype. It can be a physical object, like a sample product; a digital prototype to create an online service; or an experience prototype where explanation of a service is given. Prototyping allows working with an idea and looking for any areas that need to be tweaked in a fast and inexpensive way. At this point, the group may want to get feedback on the prototype.

Once the prototype is determined, it is time to share it with others. There are different ways to share, such as telling the story of what the prototype does. For a physical or digital prototype, an advertisement may be created; but for an experience, a skit or storyboard might be the best medium to use. After the prototype has been shared, feedback from the audience will emerge. It is important to pay attention to all forms of feedback, including body language. The next step is to reflect on the feedback and move forward to iterate.

Iteration

During the iteration stage, the prototype is refined using the information from the ideation and prototyping steps. This step can be iterated several times before moving forward. It also allows one to continue to be creative and learn from each prototype. During the iterate phase, review the three lenses – desirability, feasibility, and viability—and use them to create questions that will help with the prototype. Two or three questions per lens are necessary. From here, go back to ideation, diverge again, and then move to build the prototype.

Once confident with the prototype, it is time to move forward to pitching the idea for approval and, ultimately, creating the final product, process, or experience. Even though the design thinking process seems complex and time consuming, the process can be complete and ready to build in just a few days.

Design thinking provides a process to create ideas and move them into a final solution. By keeping the three lenses in mind, the final solution will be something that the audience will want; and the company can create within the business needs. Perhaps the hardest part of design thinking is creating the challenge statement. Being able to define the problem just right and having users in mind plus make it appealing and interesting can be difficult. The next chapter on talent acquisition strategy will address this concern.

## THREE

TALENT ACQUISITION STRATEGY WITH RELATED CHALLENGE STATEMENT

Talent Acquisition Strategy

In 2015, I was a manager of a Talent Acquisition team for a financial services company. That summer, one of our call center directors approached me and my team about a potential project for us. This project would be to set up a temporary inbound call center for about 6-9 months. We would need over 100 temp call center agents for the project. The problem was that we only had a few weeks to recruit and train the individuals before we began the project. The next issue was that we could not start sourcing and recruiting until the ink was dry on the contract. As a result, we had limited time to put together a recruiting strategy.

As the Project Lead, I needed to create:

- A fast selection process to get people in the door and hired as quickly as possible
- Recruitment marketing strategy to attract individuals to apply
- Sourcing strategy to find candidates
- Metrics and goals to ensure we hired the right amount of people in the right time frame.

The following explanation of the steps taken to complete this project is an example of Talent Acquisition Strategy.

This project was an extraordinary opportunity but an even greater challenge. Our selection process needed to be completed quickly so the team used our current process and eliminated phone screens and made offers on the spot. Working with operations allowed us to ensure that we had enough managers to interview.

The company was already recruiting call center agents. Our team used that strategy and built a new strategy focused on finding individuals who wanted temp work. The main concerns were staying within budget and ensuring the client approved the content.

Hiring in a call center environment required sourcing candidates consistently. To source the right candidates, our experienced recruiting team executed a sourcing plan, such as the following:

1. use the right keywords and built queries to pull potential candidate,
2. email candidates about the opportunity, and
3. call them.

Since it was necessary to use both email and personal contact, our motto was always "Smile and Dial."

The metrics and goals were created with the operations team. All new hires had to complete a training program before they could take any calls. Based on the capacity of our training rooms and the number of staff members needed, new hires had to be phased in. There were several new hire start dates to ensure enough people would be trained and taking calls by the start date of the new contract. In addition, the team offered day and evening training classes to ensure everyone went through training. Once the number of people for each training class was identified, key performance indicators or metrics for the team to hit based on the data for that location were provided.

The next task was getting the recruiting team in place. Since hiring was taking place in other locations as well, a system had to be created to meet this need. The solution was to create a sign up for each day, for each step of the process, and for each member of our talent acquisition team (~20) that had some sort of responsibility with this project.

All of these procedures were completed and ready to go before the project was confirmed. Obviously, these plans were risky because the project may not have materialized. On the other hand, there was a framework in place for any similar project that came our way. Operations gave the green light and the team began recruiting the same day. It was a lot of work, a lot of hours, several Saturday Open Interview Days, and a lot of travel; but hiring the number of call center agents needed was successful. The director was extremely impressed with our efforts and even nominated the whole team for a company award.

Developing a strategy to complete the project is the key. The same is true for any business; if it does not have a strategy on logistics, software, training, and so on, the project will not be successful. Therefore, having a strategy for recruiting seems to be the key to finding quality candidates and new hires successfully.

There are several different types of strategies in play when hiring—from the selection process strategy to recruitment marketing, and, finally, to the sourcing strategy. All these strategies combined create the Talent Acquisition Strategy.

The Importance of Talent Acquisition Strategy

The best CEOs understand that their business cannot grow or thrive without the right people. "Fog the mirror tests," where the interview is only confirming that the candidate can breathe, are not sufficient. A business owner should understand his/her own business needs and the appropriate resources, including talent, to meet those needs.

Hiring the wrong people can be a detriment to a business. For example, the cost of a bad hire can put a dent in the business' operating costs, especially since people are the largest investment. Talent Acquisition is not just recruiting. Talent Acquisition can provide a strategy to ensure a business can find the right people at the right time. In order for Talent Acquisition to do this, the team needs to understand the business goals and objectives, organization structure, identification of a person for the new role, and the roles needed for recruitment. The Talent Acquisition team also needs to know the timeline for this process. By having this information, the team can build a Talent Acquisition Strategy that can mirror the business' strategy.

Without a strategy, a business is just hiring to hire. There is no logic behind it. This can make turnover increase; and the waste of time, money, and resources can hurt the bottom line. A Talent Acquisition Strategy limits risk and can lower the cost of hiring, save the team's time, and boost productivity. Leaders cannot afford bad hires especially in critical roles. Steve Jobs said,

> When you're in a start-up, the first ten people will determine whether the company succeeds or not. Each is 10% of the company. So why wouldn't you take as much time as necessary to find all the A-players? If three were not so great, why would you want a company where 30% of your people are not so great? A small company depends on great people much more than a big company does."[1]

Every company starts small, so it is important to start with a Talent Acquisition strategy even when there are only a few employees. By starting with a talent acquisition strategy, a business can grow and build on that strategy. The actual process may change with time but the habit of having one is already there.

A strong talent acquisition strategy gives a competitive advantage. By hiring the right people for the right jobs, the overall productivity, customer satisfaction, and revenue will increase. And when it's time to scale or bring on a new product line, the talent acquisition team will have a strategy to hire the best talent for those new ventures.

Reasons for Starting with Talent Acquisition Strategy

When starting a new business or new product line, individuals ask whether they should go straight to building it or strategize first. It seems logical to plan first. The business strategy will include research/data, vision and mission of the organization, objectives, short-and-long term goals, and management procedures. Such a plan is part of the Talent Acquisition strategy. This strategy uses data/research to understand the climate of hiring, a mission and vision that is aligned with the business, objectives to be met to be successful, short-and-long erm goals, and metrics/KPIs to track performance. After completing the plan, the individual can start building the business.

In other words, no strategy = poor business and no talent acquisition strategy = poor hiring.

Areas of Talent Acquisition Strategy

Using the Talent Acquisition Strategy, it is best to start with a yearly strategy that can be broken down into quarterly or monthly plans. Listed below are seven items needed in the strategy:

1. Workforce Planning
2. Mission, Vision, and Goals aligned with the business
3. Employer Brand and Employee Value Proposition (EVP)
4. Candidate Attraction and Sourcing
5. Selection Process
6. Onboarding
7. Performance Metrics

Workforce Planning

When a business is forecasting and creating business initiatives, it is vital to know if the talent exists in the organization to meet the needs. Also, understanding turnover and where there may be gaps that need to be filled by a new workforce will help immensely. A better understanding of workforce planning will ensure that the talent acquisition strategy has been created to achieve the company's forecasting and business initiatives.

Alignment of Mission, Vision, and Goals with Business

At one point I had the privilege of building my talent acquisition team from scratch. When the team was developed, we sat down together virtually (since we were all over the country) and reviewed the company's mission and vision statements, and then we developed the following as our own mission and vision statements.

Our Mission: *Changing lives one Req at a time*
Our Vision: *The Talent Acquisition Team is dedicated to working collaboratively with our internal business partners by providing:*

- *exceptional representation of the company and its subsidiaries throughout our communities*
- *high quality and individualized candidate experience*
- *innovative recruiting strategies*
- *focus on the company's core values and goals.*

To accomplish these, we will ensure that the Talent Acquisition Team will recruit the best talent for the company. We will bring enthusiasm, high energy, teamwork, and creativity to work every day. And, we will have such passion for professional development and growth that it will make us the "best darn TA team ever."

The Talent Acquisition Leader worked with my peer and me in creating goals that were linked to the business goals. These goals were then broken down into the goals for each person on the team. This information was available to our business units and all of my reporting focused on these goals, as well as the business goals. We did this annually and the merit/performance review was based on this information.

The talent acquisition team needs to know and understand the mission and vision of the organization by heart and how their role ensures that the company achieves its business goals.

Employer Brand and Employee Value Proposition (EVP)

It is important to have both employer brand and employee value proposition. The employer brand can have some commonalities with the company brand. This brand will reflect the tone and feel of the content provided on the career page, job boards, social media, communication, etc. The brand focuses on the candidate's experience and the company's expectation of that experience throughout the selection process.

The Employee Value Proposition (EVP) is a combination of what is offered to the employees in return for what they bring to the table (skills, experience, knowledge, etc.). The EVP must be relevant and focused on the company, the work environment, the benefits, and the team. An EVP is not a one size fits all statement, it cannot copy another company's EVP, and it should align directly with the employer brand.

Candidate Attraction and Sourcing

What is the game plan to find, attract, and source the right type of candidates for the company? This is the proactive approach to recruiting and not a "post a position and pray" approach. This is actively searching for potential talent. But, where can the right candidates be found? Understanding the characteristics of the ideal candidate helps create a strong attraction and sourcing strategy. One way to do this is by creating a Candidate Persona. Candidate persona is taking the ideal candidate and building an avatar of the person. The Candidate Persona should be focus on the success criteria for the position. This process gives the hiring team the ability to know where to find them online, offline, etc. Using this method results in not having to use funds for sourcing tools that will not find the right candidate.

Selection Process

Are there clearly defined processes for selection? Are these processes known and understood? Building a structured selection process will streamline the work and give consistency. Also, understanding the process assists in moving the right candidates forward in the process. This is an area of potential risks; therefore, compliance and regulations must be addressed.

Onboarding

After the offer is accepted and the new hire is ready to start, is there a structured onboarding process in place? The worst-case scenario for any business is to select a person to join the organization and s/he does not start: the person declines the offer after accepting it, is a "no show" on the first day, or better yet, quits on day one.

Onboarding starts once the candidate accepts the role. It is important to continue communicating with him/her on the next steps, answering all of their questions, providing information on their onboarding, etc. The new hire needs to be kept engaged, feel the excitement of their team, and have essentials such as desk, technology, phone, and a training schedule available before they start.

Here is my onboarding horror story about one of my recruiters resigning on day one. The company I worked for acquired a business in Austin, TX; and I was going to manage recruiting for that office. Luckily, they had a recruiter already there. Unfortunately, after a few months, the recruiter decided to move on and leave the organization. I started searching for a new Recruiter. I met several candidates and provided them with tours and meetings with other leaders. It was down to two candidates. One had a lot of call center recruiting experience, from a well-known company, but did not have a lot of sourcing/passive recruiting. The other had some high volume recruiting plus military experience. I went with the individual with some high volume recruiting and military experience.

I extended the offer, and she took her time reviewing the offer at which time my intuition started telling me that this may not work out. However, she accepted so I thought maybe I was just nervous since this was a new subsidiary. Then, she also took some time to complete the background check. Again, I was concerned if this was going to work out. I kept in contact with her, and she did eventually complete everything and was ready to start.

On my flight to Austin to meet her on her first day, I still had a bad feeling about everything. I could not tell you why, but it was just that gut instinct. On my drive into the office that morning, I was really concerned that she would not start. Yet, there she was in the office. I took a big sigh of relief.

In the morning, I took her around and introduced her to all of the leaders and managers. We had a conference call with the talent acquisition team, and I started to review her training.

We headed out to lunch and had a great time. I was finally feeling more comfortable with my decision. After lunch, she took a quick call outside since it was an open office. I thought nothing of it. She came back in and told me her dream company called her and offered her a job and she accepted. Well, that was a bit shocking; but to be honest, I was relieved. My intuition was just fine. I let her leave and started my search for another recruiter.

The lesson for me was to make sure I was asking questions from my intuition and to keep that dialogue open throughout the onboarding experience.

Performance Metrics

Performance metrics need to focus on the goals set for the team. This can also include the reporting analytics for the business metrics and goals for talent acquisition. Performance metrics for the team should be reviewed monthly or quarterly. Reporting analytics can be presented quarterly, bi-yearly, as well as yearly. Chapter 9 is dedicated to metrics and analytics for talent acquisition.

Great talent acquisition teams have short-term and long-term strategies in place. They are flexible and able to shift gears when needed. They focus on the experience of all people in the selection process.

Creating a Company Challenge Statement

Defining your challenge statement is a great way to start a Talent Acquisition Strategy. First of all, an individual or company needs to understand what they want out of this strategy. Most companies use more than one of the following when developing their strategy:

- Improve cost per hire
- Reduce the time to fill
- Increase the quality of hire
- Increase the quantity of candidates

When using design thinking, the first step is defining the challenge statement. From there, the following need to be address:

1. Understanding current knowledge
2. Looking at previous years of hiring
3. Judging the current state of hiring in the company, industry, and location
4. Understanding available resources and processes
5. Knowing the team

Once this happens, additional questions may arise:

1. What are the assumptions around the challenge statement?
2. Why do these exist?
3. Why is this important?
4. What are the reasons that make this interesting?
5. What are the learnings?

Given information from this process, it is time to frame the challenge statement. This is like painting a picture of the current state of recruitment and hiring and why there is an opportunity to create a new strategy. This needs to be focused, broad enough that new areas can be discovered, manageable, and phrased as a goal.

. . .

Example of a Challenge:

Look at this like Goldie Locks – is it too big, too small, or just right? Here are some examples.

Example of a Challenge Statement focused on Increasing Quantity of Candidates:

Too big: How might we increase the number of candidates for all hiring?

Too small: How might we increase the number of candidates by 2%?

Just right: How might we increase our candidate pool by 10% in our hard to fill roles?

Example of a Challenge Statement for Time to fill:

Just right: How can we lower our time to fill from an average of 60 days to 55 days in our exempt level roles?

Example of Challenge Statement for Cost per hire:

Just right: How can we lower the cost per hire by 15% for our Cincinnati and Orlando offices?

Example of Challenge Statement for Quality of Hire:

Just right: How might we lower our new hire turnover within the first 90 days from 15% to 10%?

Following are a few tips:

- The solution should not be "baked" into the problem statement. This leaves no room for creativity.
- The challenge question should be exciting and resulting in making an impact on the business.

- The audience should be selective since the challenge and its solution is not for everyone.
- Tackling the challenge statement will be a "challenge" itself.

Once the challenge is complete, it needs to be reviewed to ensure that it draws on insights that make the challenge interesting and adds some context on the importance to the organization. Then, the challenge statement will help determine the strategy.

Building a challenge statement to create pieces of the talent acquisition strategy will keep everyone focused on the goal. It will ensure focusing on candidates, hiring managers, and company; and it will motivate the team to come up with ideas and solutions.

Templates are available to help readers with their challenge statement, talent acquisition strategy and sourcing strategy. They can be found at the end of the book and at *www.HireByDesignBook.com.*

One of the main goals of the talent acquisition strategy is to attract the right candidate pool to select the best individuals for the organization. The next chapter will focus on attraction and sourcing, as well as the employer brand, recruitment marketing, and the metrics around candidate attraction.

## FOUR

RECRUITMENT MARKETING STRATEGIES WITH STORYBOARDS

Creating a marketing strategy is key to success for a business. Understanding where to market the product or service will help a business connect with customers. For some reason, it took some time for companies to realize that they needed the same marketing plan to find candidates. Now, there are talent acquisition vendors that provide tools to develop a marketing strategy. Here is an example of one:

Phenom, a global HR technology company, partnered with RentPath, a digital media company that provides digital marketing solutions for the rental industry, to improve their employer brand and attract more candidates to grow their talent pools. The goal was to find technology that would assist their talent acquisition team in attracting, sourcing, and engaging the right talent for their company. RentPath utilized the Phenom Talent Experience Management platform. This system provided them with a career site focused on their employer brand plus technology to assist with identifying potential candidates and engaging them with email campaigns. All of this was done in one location.

Within 90 days, RentPath's leads from their campaign increased by 580%, applications from their campaign increased by 246%, and the company received 962 applications from 87 job postings. Their career site analytics improved as well as the candidate analytics for their talent pool.

By asking the question (challenge statement), "how can we improve our employer brand and attract more candidates to grow our talent pool?", Rent-Path was able to start exploring options and find the right option that provided a strong return on investment (ROI). The right option focused on the candidate experience by creating a personalized approach and focused on the recruiter by providing a platform that was easy to use and that saved time.

In order to be able to achieve these types of results, RentPath needed to understand their targeted candidate pool, create a strong employer brand, and know how to attract that group.[1]

Employer Branding

Most companies focus on their company brand to attract customers; however, the employer brand helps the company attract the right talent. Further, the employer brand can be an extension of the company's brand, but it needs to highlight what the company stands for as an employer, why someone should work for them, and what the work environment/culture is like. In order to have a strong employer brand, selection of the right talent is important. So many companies just play the numbers game, i.e., get as many candidates to apply as possible and then sift through them until the best talent is identified.

High volume recruiting that focuses on entry-level roles can play the numbers game, but it is not a great solution. Typically, having specific experience is not needed in entry-level roles because the candidates often get all the experience they need through training. Therefore, lots of people can do a given job. However, people who can do the job are not always what the company needs. They need individuals who meet the following criteria:

Learn Quickly	Follow Guidelines	Are Reliable	Have a Good Work Ethic

Hiring just anyone for the role can jeopardize the work environment, performance, and retention. The story below is an example of entry-level hiring and recruitment strategies.

Early in my career, I was recruiting for a call center where they trained all their call center agents. Anyone who had at least a high school diploma or GED that could pass our background check was an ideal candidate for us. We were hiring 10 to 15 agents every 2 weeks. In order to do that, we allowed individuals to come into our office, apply, interview, and generally get an offer on the spot. We joked that it was the "fog the mirror" interview. As long as the candidate could breathe, s/he got the job. Were we able to hire the 10 to 15 agents every two weeks? Yes, we were able to do this. Yet, did they all work out? No, they did not. Some did not even make it to the first day, some did not make it through the first week, some did not make it through the 3-week training, and some did not make it through the first 90 days. There were always some great hires who were successful and got promoted in the call center. But that was not the norm.

We needed to understand more fully the type of person who was the best candidate for this role. We needed to come up with an employer brand and a recruitment marketing strategy to target those individuals so that when individuals came in to interview, there was a higher probability for them to be successful.

We did eventually add a pre-employment assessment to our process and completed a job analysis and validation to ensure that it would help us with hiring the right candidates. This did help. But when you are hiring entry-level, there is always a chance that it will not work out even with the best candidates. It is just a part of the life of entry-level hiring.

Thus, the goal is to attract the right talent through your employer brand by painting a picture of the organization, explaining what the team does, and providing the values of the organization. The employer brand includes the following:

Recruitment Marketing	Social Media	Career Site
Talent Communities	Communication	Job Postings

To create the employer brand, the following topics need to be addressed:

1. *Knowledge of the company*

    a. An explanation of the company in a few sentences
    b. An understanding by the team of what the company does or what the business objectives are
    c. Knowledge of the Mission, Vision, and Values
    d. Knowledge of the work environment and culture

2. *Knowledge of the employees*

    a. Identification of the bottom, middle, and top talent – who are they, what is their background, how did they learn about the role, etc.
    b. Employee longevity – Why do employees stay? Why do employees

leave? What do exit surveys reveal? What information was provided in the stay surveys?

c. Qualifications of a great candidate – What do managers look for in a great candidate? What do leaders want for a workforce?

d. An employee value proposition – What is special about the company? What do they offer their employees for their performance, skills, and experience?

3. *Knowledge of the candidates*

a. *Creation of candidate personas* that provide insight into the ideal candidates

- What does their background look like: education, experience, skills, etc.?
- Focus on success factors and not demographics information like specific school that may exclude underrepresented candidates who fit the success factors.
- Where are they online? Social Media, news, industry-specific, or role-specific websites
- Where are they offline? Areas of the country that they live, places they go, people they see, etc.
- What motivates them? Money, culture, benefits, interesting projects, etc.

b. *Creation of a competitor's analysis*

- Where do the ideal candidates work and why?
- What is the competitor doing to attract the same candidate pool?
- What makes the competitor different from the company identified? What makes the identified company different from the competitor?

c. *Company Reputation* – What are people saying about the company (customers, experts, employees, and candidates)? This is the information candidates see when they do research.

- The good
- The bad
- The ugly

4. *Strategy*

a. How will ideal candidates be identified through marketing?

- Online
- Offline

b. How will communication to the ideal candidates of the employer brand and employee value proposition take place?
c. How will the team, managers, and employees engage to assist with recruitment?

5. *Company Brand*

a. The employer brand needs to be aligned with the company brand. How will this be accomplished?
b. The marketing team can assist with alignment of the employer brand and the company brand.

6. *KPIs (Key Performance Indicators)*

a. What will be the indicator that the new employer brand and strategy are working?

Recruitment Marketing

Recruitment marketing is a strategy often used to attract and engage job seekers through various marketing strategies. Readers may use the information in this book to create a similar marketing strategy to use to obtain customers or clients. Instead of attracting customers or clients, however, the goal will be to attract candidates and future employees.

Recruitment
Marketing

A comparison of hiring practices and the shape of a funnel shows that recruitment marketing is at the very top of the funnel —that is, at the largest part of the funnel. Attracting a lot of potential candidates will allow the right candidates to go down to the next step of the funnel which means they become an applicant.

The recruiter needs to start looking at the best practices for digital marketing, such as reputation, management, outreach, and communication and engagement. Also, it is important to use the candidate persona for the recruitment marketing. The candidate persona will help identify a strategy that will pinpoint the places to find specific candidates. Depending on the situation, it is possible to create several candidate personas for the company, department, and jobs. These candidate personas will help determine marketing strategies that focus on where to advertise. If the persona uses Instagram for their social media feed, utilize paid targeted ads on Instagram. Creating a free business page on Facebook will allow content about the employer brand and hiring initiatives to appear. Since the persona uses Instagram more, paid targeted advertisement on Facebook is not necessary. Funds should be used where there is the best return on an investment.

Another way to focus the budget is through programmatic advertising. This type of advertising allows the company to buy ad space to target the ideal candidate or to retarget individuals who went to the career site but did not actually apply. When a computer user views a couch online and then has ads for that exact couch appear all over the internet, that phenomenon is created using programmatic ad buying and retargeting.

Another approach to recruitment marketing is inbound marketing— focusing on generating leads through content marketing, search engine optimization, and social media marketing. Inbound marketing focuses on the candidate and provides him/her with information to solve problems or complete tasks that will attract them to the company. Blogging about different parts of the hiring process like "Interview Best Practices" or "Top 5 Tips for Your Resume" is an effective way to provide content to candidates that is free. It is also a vehicle to capture the individual's information and to allow joining the talent pool. Content should be distributed regularly if it is to rank high in the search engines, keep the engagement on social media, boost followers, and be recognized as an influencer. The goal is to stay in front of the candidate persona, provide good content which ensures remembrance, and give outlets to stay connected via following your social media, getting your newsletter, etc.

Social Media

Social Media Recruiting consists of a business page displayed on social media sites like LinkedIN and FaceBook, job postings, and targeted job ads.

A business page should have information about the employee value proposition, the employees/work environment, and job openings. Content used for other inbound marketing campaigns can also be included. Leaders and anyone who helps with recruiting can add content and provide answers to questions from potential candidates.

Job postings can be added to the business page, job search groups, and the team's social media pages. Providing the content to employees is one way to help ensure that they post it. It also contributes to the employer brand or company brand focus.

Targeted job ads can engage passive candidates. Most social media channels offer this. When using targeted job ads, the candidate personas should be targeted and there should be interesting information provided for them. Tracking the ads will help in determining their effectiveness.

Career Site and Talent Communities

The recruitment marketing strategy will get potential candidates to the career site. This is the main hiring site for the organization. This will have information on the company—benefits, values, culture, EVP, open positions, etc.

According to a recent Talent Board survey, job seekers spend one to four hours researching companies, and 65% of them found the career site to be the most helpful resource.[2] When designing a career site, it should be easy to use and provide all the information the candidates want in one spot.

On average, only 10% of individuals who go to a career site apply, so there needs to be a strategy to ensure engaging the 90% who do not apply. Creating a talent community where someone can put their contact information with the type of role they are looking for is a great way to capture their information. Having a talent community is part of an inbound marketing strategy, meaning engaging them through content and communication. This strategy helps determine whether the candidate is a good fit for the organization.

The career site should be fluid; updated regularly with new information, like employee testimonials, or photos from employee events, etc; and reviewed either quarterly or bi-yearly for any updates and enhancements.

Communication

Communication is so important to hiring that it has its own chapter in this book. Consistent communication is key. Communication through inbound marketing needs to be consistent with the employer brand and employee value proposition. The communication should not be redundant but can be similar if using different channels. The talent community also needs to be communicated consistently, including touchpoints from the recruiter to blog information to company announcements.

Today during the Covid-19 pandemic, communicating to potential candidates, current candidates, and new hires is extremely important. They need to be informed about the following:

- How are the company and employees doing?
- What has changed because of this?
- Is the company currently hiring?

- If not, how will they be informed when hiring begins again?
- If yes, what has changed in the selection and interview process?

- What is their status? Are they still in the process?
- Are there any changes with onboarding for new hires?

It is essential to keep potential candidates informed and to let them know they are important. These candidates need to be kept in the loop just as much as the employees.

Job Postings

When is the last time that you looked at a job posting? Experience has revealed that when talking to individuals searching for a job, one of their top three complaints is about the job posting.

Their complaints include:

1. Too Vague – no clue what the role is or what they will be doing every day
2. Too Much – too much information or too many job requirements
3. No What's in it for me (WIIFM)– what does the company offer their employees? (Employer Branding!)
4. Salary Information – how much will I make…job seekers prefer not to apply to roles that are beneath their pay grade
5. Job Description – the job description is written to the company's needs, not the candidates.

When putting together a job posting, some essential elements need to be included: company information, daily responsibilities, minimum job requirements (skills, experience, education), compensation, and the employee value proposition. It should be easy to read and encourage the candidates to apply.

Compensation can be hard to include because some job seekers may take advantage of having this information. However, conducting a compensation analysis and taking into consideration the amount of experience needed should attract candidates who are within the given range plus a few who are below the range. It might also encourage individuals who might be hesitant to apply. The analysis should also help determine anyone who is not at the level needed and if the compensation is not enough. The individuals who want more money typically meet and exceed expectations; but if these candidates are introduced to the manager, the hiring manager usually wants to hire them but cannot because they are not in the compensation range. This is the time things usually get hairy. Once a manager sees an A+++ candidate who is above the compensation, it is hard for him/her to go back to reality and select an A candidate that will take the posted compensation. Generally, it means starting the process over.

Attracting Talent with Storyboards

Creating a storyboard to tell the story of the candidate experience can showcase how it will fit into the candidate's life. Storyboards provide a method of sharing ideas in a quick and virtual way, and they can tell the story about solving the challenge statement by describing who benefits from the solution. It also focuses on their actions, emotions, thoughts, goals, and relationships. When creating a story board, the process is similar to brainstorming. There will be time limits so that the team can focus on creating multiple ideas for the storyboard in a short amount of time. As in brainstorming, ideas are recorded on paper or post-it notes before discussing them. Discussion ensues and ideas are clustered to determine patterns. Once clustered, it is time to converge and identify the best ideas. By using improvisation and saying "Yes, and...", the team will ensure all ideas are reviewed and included in the discussion. The following is an example of a storyboard created by the author.

While taking a class through IDEO U, I created a storyboard for an idea I had for public libraries to attract more children to the library and encourage more reading. The idea was to have an app that parents and children can use to encourage reading and utilizing public libraries.

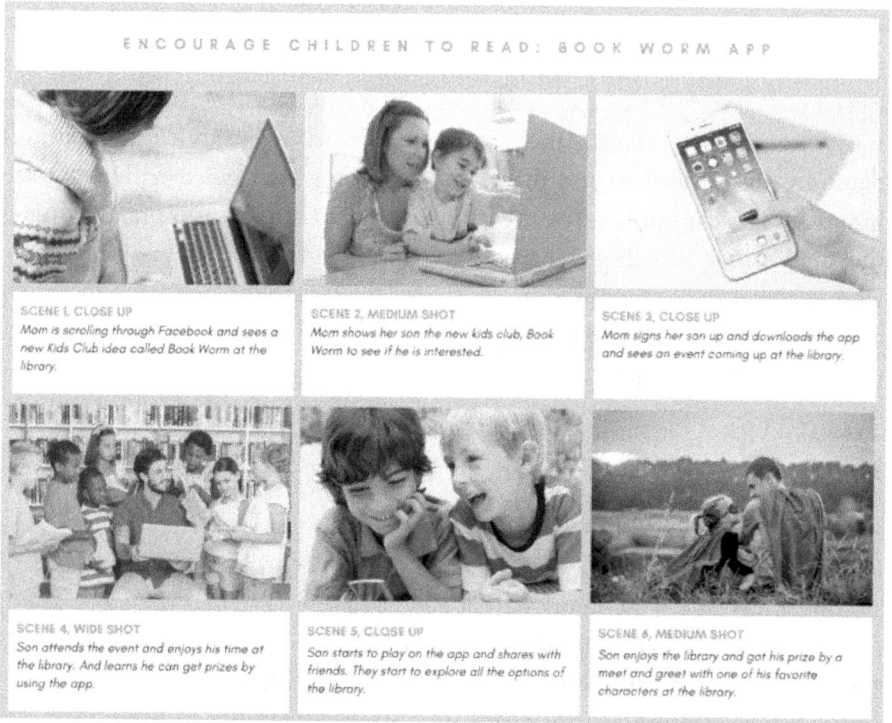

ENCOURAGE CHILDREN TO READ: BOOK WORM APP

SCENE 1, CLOSE UP
Mom is scrolling through Facebook and sees a new Kids Club idea called Book Worm at the library.

SCENE 2, MEDIUM SHOT
Mom shows her son the new kids club, Book Worm to see if he is interested.

SCENE 3, CLOSE UP
Mom signs her son up and downloads the app and sees an event coming up at the library.

SCENE 4, WIDE SHOT
Son attends the event and enjoys his time at the library. And learns he can get prizes by using the app.

SCENE 5, CLOSE UP
Son starts to play on the app and shares with friends. They start to explore all the options of the library.

SCENE 6, MEDIUM SHOT
Son enjoys the library and got his prize by a meet and greet with one of his favorite characters at the library.

The goal of a storyboard is to focus on the candidates and tell their story and not the company story. The candidate should be the center of attention. In groups or individually, the candidate is created using the candidate persona. Sketches with speech and thought bubbles, action bursts, captions, and narratives emerge. The candidate now has his/her own comic strip! Each group or person shows their storyboards, and common threads are identified.

Here are a few ideas for developing a storyboard to help with attracting talent:

1. A Candidate Navigating the Career Site to Apply
2. Creating blog posts that target the pain points for specific candidates
3. A Candidate asks a question about benefits via social media
4. The story of re-targeting the ideal candidate via ads

5. Story of engaging candidates after they join the talent community

Attracting ideal candidates through employer branding is all about understanding who the ideal candidates are, where to find them, and how to talk to them. Storyboards are all about the user's experience. A storyboard can help paint a picture of ways to attract candidates based on the people targeted. It is an easy and fast way to make sure the candidate experience works for the candidate persona. There is a Candidate Persona and Job Posting template at the end of the book and at *www.HireByDesignBook.com.*

The next chapter will discuss the selection process, the different steps in the process, and ways smash up for ideation can benefit the selection process.

## FIVE

SELECTION PROCESS WITH MASH-UP TECHNIQUE

Selection Process

The selection process is a series of steps that a candidate completes in order to be hired. Many companies use the same selection process for years; however, as a company changes, the selection process must be reviewed and updated. If a process is kept too long, it may no longer work for the company. Following is an example:

One of my clients wanted to update their pre-employment assessment because of the length of the assessment. They were also not using all the data provided from the assessment. They used two different assessment tools and a candidate had to complete them in two steps. Also, they needed an Industrial Organizational (I/O) Psychologist to review and interpret the results. That same I/O Psychologist spent four hours with the candidate once they were invited onsite for an interview. That was a lot of time for a candidate to be completing an assessment, plus it added time to the overall selection process.

The result was that they not only needed a new pre-employment assessment, but they also needed to update their selection process. Their current selection process took a candidate at least 25 hours to complete, and the total time between steps would be between 23 to 30+ days. By updating the selection process and pre-employment assessment, the candidate's time was reduced to 14 hours, and the total time between steps was 19-24 days. Thus, 11 hours of the candidate's time were removed, and the number of days between steps were reduced by 4 to 6 days. This process ensured that the interview team and candidate had all the information they needed to make a good, sound decision, and the process reflected the company's culture.

A selection process is just as important as attracting the right talent. It is a part of the employer brand, as well as the company's culture. Ideally, the selection process should be reviewed yearly to ensure it meets the needs and is candidate friendly.

Steps of the Selection Process

A selection process may have one step or more than 15 steps. The number of steps depends on the information needed to make a good hiring decision for the company. Also, there may be a few steps that are required by regulations or by employment law that must be added as well. Here are the common steps to the selection process:

Create a job, job description, job posting

Review Resumes/Applications--decide based on resume if candidate moves forward

Pre-screen/ One-way Video--provide questions for the candidate to answer based on the role and requirements

Phone Screen--15-20 minute interview over the phone completed by HR, Recruiter, or Hiring Manager

Pre-employment assessment--tools to evaluate the candidate's capabilities and ability to perform the role

Phone Interview--more in-depth interview by phone

Onsite Interview/Video interview--face to face interview with hiring manage and key stake holders.

Panel Interview--group completes the interview

Tour--physical tour of the building or virtual tour

Job Shadow --allow candidate to sit with someone who has the same or similar role

Technical Interview--determines candidates skills in technology

Lunch Interview--casual interview over lunch

Business Case--provides scenario for candidate to present findings or solution

Evaluation of candidate--Feedback from all on the candidate

Offer approval--obtaining approval to extend offer

Background Check--based on requirements of the company

References--responses from professional and personal references

Offer extended--verbal and written offer to candidate

Start date--establish start date for new hire

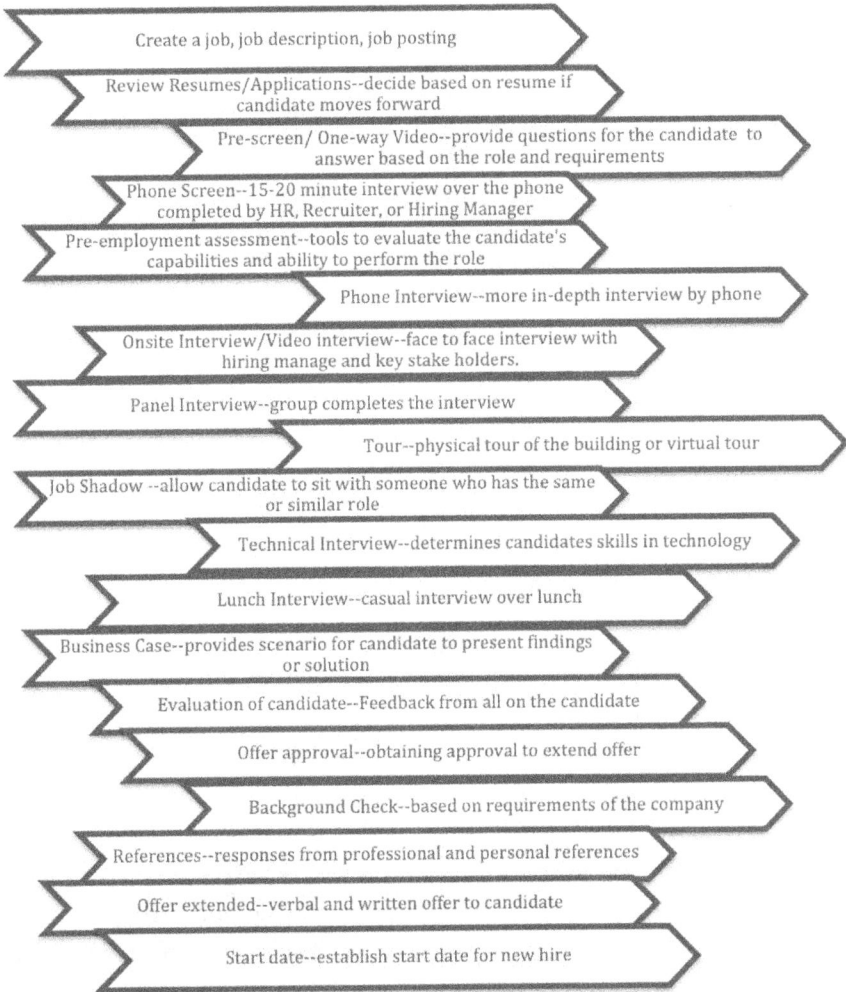

Companies need to have back up plans when they create their selection process. They may have to move an onsite interview to a video interview, for example, or make sure that the process meets ADA guidelines, as well as any regulations/employment law requirements.

The following is a list of the basics needed in the selection process:

1. Create a detail job description and job posting that highlights the responsibili-

ties, day to day activities, and provides the requirements needed to perform the role.

When creating the job description and job posting, attention should be focused on whom the company wants to target to ensure finding the right candidates and making the right hiring decision. Not knowing exactly what type of person is needed will result in focusing the recruitment marketing to the wrong candidate persona and necessitate starting over. Obviously, this will add additional time to hire, or the company hires someone who does not fit the profile. At this point, the following will probably happen: change the role, train the person, or let the person go, resulting in lower performance.

It is important to take time creating the job details. Ask the following questions.

- What experience, skills or education should the candidate bring with them in order to be successful in this role?
- What skills can the company provide training for and still make sure that the candidate is successful?

2. List the avenues to find candidates: recruitment marketing, post online, internal job postings, etc.

What is the best way to find the right candidates? The candidate persona will help here. Finding the right candidate requires looking both inside and outside the company. Finding an internal candidate will lower the amount of training needed and can boost employee morale. For example, hiring recruiters requires training them on the company or recruiting. Sometimes training on recruiting is easier than training on the company.

3. Note the avenues for candidates to show interest — career site, email, text, phone, voice, bot

Once someone is interested in the role, the next step is to find an easy way to get information about the person. Typically, companies will ask for a resume and/or application. A pet peeve of candidates is the situation in which they are asked for their resume and then asked to complete an application with the exact same information required. The solution is to find a tool that can parse their resume information into the application or wait until a later time or a different step to ask for the application to be completed.

The company should be open to allowing a potential candidate to email or call to ask questions about the role before applying. If they are interested, they will apply through the career site. Some candidates want a little more information before they do apply, and some of these candidates may be the best candidates for the role. There are even text tools out there where individuals can apply. In fact, there is even voice command tools like Siri or Alexa that work for candidates to apply. It is all about what is best for the candidates (aka candidate persona) and the business.

4. Review candidates' credentials (resume review, prescreen, assessment, etc.)

What information is needed to confirm moving forward with a candidate? Is it just reviewing the resume? Are there a few questions candidates need to answer either through a pre-screen or one-way video? Are there technical skills that need to be confirmed through a technical assessment? Or are there behaviors that need to be evaluated through a behavioral assessment?

When deciding on the steps to review the candidate's credentials, these steps must stay the same for each candidate applying to the same position. When reviewing candidates for the same role, one must review each candidate in the same manner. In addition, the assessment must be based on the requirements for the role. For example, a Call Center Agent should not take an Excel Assessment if he/she will not be using Excel. There is no need to make candidates "jump through hoops" that give no information on how they will perform for their role.

5. Interview candidates either over the phone, video, or onsite

Choosing the best method of interviewing candidates depends on logistics. A phone interview may be the best way to start the interview process and then move to a video or onsite interview. If hiring at a high volume, going straight to onsite interviewing may be the best. To ensure that candidates are not required to do unnecessary steps, the interviewers should pay attention to how many times a candidate completes an interview and should ensure that each interview generates new information.

Also, the interview team should understand their role and the characteristics of the ideal candidate. A structured interview guide can help with the interview, and the same guide should be used with all candidates interviewed for that role. This process guarantees that all candidates are being evaluated with the same information.

The team that the person will be working with needs to be a part of the process. They should be part of the decision and feel confident in the person joining them. The team can be a part of the onsite interview by completing a panel interview, lunch, tour of the office, or job shadow. This will also help with onboarding and, hopefully, create a positive work environment in the process.

6. Evaluate candidate to decide to hire or not – everyone involved gets a say

An evaluation form will help the interviewers with evaluating all the candidates. If they are a part of the interview team, they need to provide their feedback. This should be an easy form to fill out.

7. Extend offer with official letter (ensure compliant with ADA/employment law/regulations – ensure compensation is correct with compensation analysis)

The offer letter is a legal document. Anything that is included in it needs to be compliant with employment laws and regulations affecting the company. Also, the letter needs to have all the details to help the person be ready to start. This can be their start date, start time, where to go on their first day, dress code, etc. This information can be included in the offer letter or attached. To create an offer letter template, there are examples online. Getting an attorney to review is highly encouraged.

When extending an offer, ensuring a competitive compensation is necessary for an offer acceptance. In order to know if the offer is competitive, a compensation analysis is needed. A compensation analysis reviews similar roles in the same proximity and provides a compensation range. When making the final decision on compensation, a review of internal employees in similar roles and their compensation will help with internal equity.

Generally, the goal is to get an offer acceptance within the first offer. Counteroffers are an option but are not recommended. If offer countering is part of the process, obtaining approval for the highest amount to offer up front is encouraged. No need to delay the offer due to red tape.

Clients looking for sales professionals seem to like counteroffers. The hiring manager wants his sales team to be good at negotiations. Counteroffers are negotiations. The hiring manager also understands time is of the essence. He gets a compensation approval for the target salary plus approval for the max salary. Obviously, this method saves time. On the other hand, if this process is not available, there needs to be another method. In this case, if an offer is extended and the candidate counters, a discussion with the hiring manager would allow consideration of the counteroffer and it may be approved the same day or next day.

8. Consider a background check—if required or based on company preference

Background checks should be reviewed by an attorney because there have been so many federal, state, county, and city changes on what can and cannot be completed in a background check. Only pertinent information is needed so do not include credit checks, for example, if they are not needed. Requiring a background check can change based on the duties of the job. If hiring an A/P clerk and s/he needs a High School Diploma or equivalent, there is really no need to confirm education. Whereas, if hiring an Information Security Analyst and s/he needs a CISSP certification, confirming the certification makes sense.

The other piece to pay attention to is the amount of time it takes to complete the background check. If the process is too long, candidates may continue to interview, receive another offer, and not start. Right now, with the pandemic, a lot of courthouses are either closed or have limited staff. This can delay criminal background checks. Allowing someone to start contingent on the background check will help with limiting the time it takes for someone to start.

During weather related delays like hurricanes or tornados, there can also be delays on criminal backgrounds. This is no one's fault. Sometimes, the hiring team can get approval to hire individuals contingent upon receipt of the check; but the new hire has to be informed that if anything that s/he did not disclose shows up, s/he may be terminated. It was up to them to wait or start. There should always be a backup plan.

9. Determine Onboarding/Start Date – welcome new team member and ensure readiness to start.

The time between the offer acceptance and starting date is the time that many companies drop the ball. They allow that individual to just wait in silence, resulting in the candidate having a great deal of anxiety regarding their career search. Once they are at the end of it, their anxiety can decrease or increase, based on how the onboarding process works.

Below is a list of everything needed between the offer and start date. Here is a nice framework to use.

- Communication Plan

  - Provide information regarding background checks and references. Have they been cleared?
  - Discussion on expectations for the first day—and even the first week
  - Welcome from the hiring manager and time for additional questions to him/her
  - Follow-up phone calls or emails the day before they start to let them know how excited the team is for them to start and see if they have any last-minute questions.

- Preparation

  - Provide them with any documents or forms that they can complete prior to their start date.
  - Give information about any videos or company information that they can be reviewing during this time

- Check that the hiring manager has everything ready for the new hire, including office/cubicle, technology, phone, training schedule, etc.

By creating a strong selection process, companies will be able to hire the best talent in a timely fashion and ensure that candidates are engaged and excited to join the team.

Candidates typically state that the selection process is long, tedious, and sometimes not worth the time. Some people refuse to even apply to certain companies because they do not want to deal with the process. When it is time to revamp the selection process, coming up with creative and new ideas will help take an outdated, overly complicated process to one focused on the candidate.

The "Mash Up" Technique

A "mash up" is one way to do an ideation session. It involves putting two completely different, odd, or unexpected things together to spark fresh ideas. But, to do this, there must be a "How Might We" challenge statement.[1]

Here is an example:

Let's go with "how might we make our selection process more focused on the candidates' needs". Now pick two broad, unrelated categories like Dating AND Interviewing. Start with one category and list as many elements about that category in 1 to 2 minutes. The following list is an example for both categories created in 2 minutes:

Dating:	Interviewing:
Matchmaking	Phone
Online match making sites	Video
Dinner	In person
Dates	Panel
No Show	Behavioral Interview Questions
Ghost	Q&A session
Not what I though via profile	Get to know you
Blind Date	Time between each interview
Gifts	No Show
Get to know you	Bias
Kissing	Boring
Rejection	Listening
Phone Calls	Rejection
Texting	Love
Meeting friends	Meeting the teams
Meeting Parents	Tour of Office
I love you	Too many
Rose color glasses	Too long

After generating the list, combine one from each category and start brainstorming. The brainstorming session can be as fast as a few minutes to 20 to 30 minutes.

Below are a few ideas from brainstorming the selection "Dates and Too Many Interviews." When dating we want lots of dates because each one takes us to the next level of a relationship. Interviews feel dry, boring, and each one seems to be the same. Here are some ideas from the mash up:

- Food: The interview or conversation can be during a meal – breakfast, lunch, dinner.
- Change of Scenery: Conduct an interview while walking around the office or outside, in a conference room, in the breakroom, etc.
- Have each interview move you forward in the process the same as you would in dating – example: Meet the Manager, Tour the office or take a virtual tour of company, Meet the Team, Meet the leaders. Let the candidate know that each new step means they are moving forward in the process. You will not move them forward if they are not the best candidate or someone you are interested in.

at whole brainstorming session took only about 10 minutes. The mash up technique is a pretty easy way to get some new ideas fast.

---

e selection process may make or break the talent acquisition strategy. Ensuring that the process meets the needs of the business, as well as the candidate needs, the team may revisit the process and update based on changes in the company or with the world. The process needs to be flexible to accommodate any changes that happen, such as weather-related emergencies, pandemics, etc. Regardless, a technique, such as a mash up ideation session, will help create fresh new ideas for the selection process. Within the templates provided at the end of the book and at *www.HireByDesignBook. com*, there is an onboarding checklist and mash up session sheet.

Talent acquisition technology can also help solve issues within the selection processes, as well as other parts of the talent acquisition strategy. The amount of options is endless. For example, a great brainstorming ideation session may just do the trick in selecting a new talent acquisition technology. The talent acquisition technology and brainstorming will be discussed more fully in the next chapter.

## SIX

TALENT ACQUISITION TECHNOLOGY AND BRAINSTORMING

Talent Acquisition Technology

The number of systems available for Talent Acquisition and Human Resources technology is overwhelming. Finding just the right tool among these can take a lot of time and energy.

One of my clients was looking for a new pre-employment assessment. At the time, they were using an assessment that was time consuming, needed an Industrial Organizational (I/O) psychologist to review, and provided information that was not linked to their core competencies. Ideally, they wanted a fun, easy to use assessment that the team could interpret, that provided key findings aligned with their core competencies, and that matched their culture. My two-hour research for the client yielded over 80 potential assessments.

Following the research, I had to complete the following steps:

- reviewed 77 assessment vendors via their website and any additional information online,

- selected 16 to interview and demo their assessment tool, and
- selected two potential assessment vendors for my client to review.

My approach to this project included several pieces of design thinking, including creating a challenge statement, interviewing based on what my client wanted from the assessment, coming up with insights, and brainstorming for ideation. During my interviews and demos, it was relatively easy for me to find two tools that would work for my client. Listed below are the two assessments, with Assessment #1 being my safe option.

Assessment #1:

- Similar to the current assessment
- Took less time and easier for the candidate to complete
- Vendor information easier for my client to interpret.

Assessment #2:

- Alignment with their culture and work environment
- Focus on solving problems through a "gamify" approach
- Fun and easy for the candidate to complete
- Overall results that client could interpret
- Candidates have access to their results immediately upon completion of the assessment

After reviewing both assessments, my client chose the 2nd assessment – *pymetrics*. Pymetrics "helps companies better understand their workforce while making better and fairer people decisions with behavioral science and ethical AI technology."[1] Pymetrics was founded by Frida Polli, PhD. During an interview with Frida, she stated that she started pymetrics because after being a part of the recruitment process during her MBA studies, she saw several points of failure in the hiring process where the lack of job fit was the main issue. She saw her peers play the interview game by studying and preparing for the interview to realize after a few days at the company, the role was not a fit. By using neuroscience and machine learning, pymetrics can match individuals to the right role.[2]

Having a user-center design is important to the goals of pymetrics. In the same interview, Frida

stated that "the neuroscience games were created in academia and were clunky and not user friendly. Pymetrics took those games and designed the experience to be user friendly."[3]

To ensure all of their products are user-centric, pymetrics established the Candidate Advisory Council to test products and provide feedback. Frida provided advice to companies that are looking at purchasing new technology; and she said, "Do not just look at the process when selecting technology. The key is to find a system that provides data insight on all levels of the company, from candidates to the workforce, that can then drive decisions and action."[4]

Selecting talent acquisition and HR technology is no easy task; but every company needs to understand fully the benefits of technology, its appropriate application in their company and selection process, and its impact on the people using it (hiring manager, recruiter, candidate) and the selection process.

Talent Acquisition Technology can be arranged into several categories from sourcing to engagement to select and hire/onboarding.

Source Technology

Source technology provides the tools to find active and passive candidates. This includes job boards, job board aggregators, programmatic advertising, social media, referral program systems, and online staffing tools.

Job boards are places where positions can be posted and resumes sourced. Job board aggregators provide job posting capabilities, as well as sourcing resumes. Source technology would also include programmatic advertising, social networks, and social searches. Another sourcing technology is a referral program system where employees and friends of the company can provide resumes of potential candidates. Referrals can come from employees, clients, candidates, or fans of the company. There are also online staffing tools for sourcing. Those include crowdsourcing to recruiter marketplace and staffing, both temporary and direct.

Examples of Sourcing Technology

Job Boards	CareerBuilder	Dice	Ladders
Job Board Aggregators	Indeed	Simply Hired	NEXXT
Programmatic Advertising	Recruitics	Appcast	
Social Media Networks:	LinkedIN	Facebook	Stack Overflow
Social Search:	Zapinfo	Entelo	Hiretual
Referral Programs:	Teamable	ROIKOI	
Crowdsourcing:	99designs	Zoopa	
Recruiting Marketplace:	Reflik	Scout	
Staffing:	Tilr	Upwork	Talent.io

Engagement Technology

Engagement technology is a tool to engage potential candidates to active candidates. Employer branding comes into play with this technology. This includes Employer Brand Management and Job Post Optimization. These tools will ensure employer brand is present in everything that is online, as well as optimizing job postings to attract the ideal candidate. Employer review sites are also included in Employer Brand tools. Communication tools keep companies in front of the candidates by using messaging, email, text, bots, etc. A great deal of automation and artificial intelligence exists within this area. When engaging candidates, Candidate Relationship Management is needed. This is similar to a Client Relationship Management system for sales but focused on the candidate relationship.

Examples of Engagement Technology

Employer Brand Management:	The Muse	Brazen	
Job Post Optimization:	Textio	Jobcast	
Employer Review Sites:	GlassDoor	Vault	
Communication Tools:	TextRecruit	Herefish	AllyO
Candidate Relationship Management:	Smashfly	Phenom People	Talemtry

Select Technology

Select tools are incorporated in the selection process. There is matching technology that will help match candidates to the right position, as well as resume parsing software to add candidate information into the applicant tracking system. This is also another area that relies heavily on automation and artificial intelligence. In the interviewing piece of the selection process, there are tools that incorporate interview management and video interviewing. There are two different types of assessments – skill and behavioral – that can be included in the selection process. Some vendors provide both.

Examples of Select Technology

Matching Technology:	Ideal	Recruitbot
Resume Parsing:	eGrabber	Textkernel
Interview Management:	Convey	Interviewer
Video Interviewing:	Wepow	Spark hire
Skill Assessments:	Verve	HackerRank
Behavioral Assessments:	pymetrics	Predictive Index

Hire/Onboarding Technology

Hiring and onboarding technology focuses on completing the hiring and moving the candidates into an employee status. To complete hiring, most companies complete a reference and background check. Tools that help with this include reference check tools and background check tools. Applicant Tracking, Vendor Management, and Freelance Management Systems keep track of candidates, staffing agencies, contractors, or freelancers. Each system assists with a different type of hiring. Also, analytics tools are included in this section.

Examples of Hire/Onboarding Technology

Reference Checks:	Crosschq	SkillSurvey	
Background Checks:	Sterling	Checkr	Accurate
Applicant Tracking:	Workable	Workday	Lever
Vendor Management:	VNDLY	Skillstream	
Freelance Management:	Talon	JobBliss	
Analytics:	Brightfield	Talentegy	talenytics

To find an extensive list of the different Talent Technology, go to *www.talenttechlabs.com/digital-ecosystem*.

There are some vendors who have several different tools that can be used throughout the talent acquisition strategy. Businesses want to ensure that they are making the best decision for their company and get a return on investment.

An example of a vendor with multiple tools is ULIMI. ULIMI provides Human Resources Technology that saves business time and money including ULIMI Hire, a chatbot for pre-screening candidates and answering questions, ULIMI Reach, text messaging communication tool and other human resource technology for on-boarding, retention and exit interviews.[5]

When adding new technology, obtaining feedback from everyone who will be working with this technology is crucial. Including key stakeholders (i.e., candidates, talent acquisition, or HR team and management) will ensure buy in and create an easy process to implement the new technology.

Ensuring Return on Investment on Talent Acquisition Technology

First, the technology must align with the talent acquisition strategy. What are the goals for the strategy and how can technology help with those goals? It is important to

- review each initiative and rank them to decide where to start,
- look at which initiative will bring the most bang for the buck, and
- look at which ones will be touched by the most people and can be used frequently.

Technology is not cheap. Most companies ask for at least a one-year commitment. There is a risk that the technology will not provide the return on investment. Therefore, one should look for technology that has data analytics and reporting included in the system. Tracking the performance of the technology will provide helpful insight on whether this technology is producing the results needed.

When making the decision to use technology versus manual (aka human), the question emerges: "Will technology make the process, candidate experience, and the team better?" There are times when technology is not the best fit, so it should be considered in terms of whether it will enhance a team to do a better job.

The following scenario gives an example of a situation in which someone wants a personal touch in the process. There are so many times that a candidate receives an automated thanks but no thanks letter, and they can tell instantly that it was automated and not written directly to him/her. How do you think a boyfriend or girlfriend would feel if she/he is broken up with by using an automated response? It would not be pleasant. So why are companies breaking up with candidates using this method? Time is a critical factor and technology saves money; however, somehow the technology and human touch need to be combined during the process—both for the candidate and the recruiters.

Brainstorming

Brainstorming is a creative strategy for teams to generate ideas when they are trying to come up with quick potential solutions to a challenge. For example, a team is looking to add a new tool to a process. By understanding the challenge or what the tool is going to solve, the team can do a brainstorming session to come up with ideas on the type of tool or which vendor to review.

A well-organized brainstorming session is needed for anything to get accomplished. The team must have a space where there are no distractions; a designated person to be the timekeeper and facilitator so that s/he can keep the group focused; materials, such as post-it notes, markers, and a blank wall for recording ideas; and a decision regarding whether the brainstorming will be completed individually or in groups. If the process uses groups, they should be no larger than 5 or 6 people.

Understanding the rules is the first step. Following are rules provided by IDEO U.

1. Provide a specific number of minutes to brainstorm.

   a. Ten minutes is good start.
   b. The timekeeper needs to keep the groups informed on the amount of time left. This gives a sense of urgency.

2. Generate as many ideas as possible—the good, the bad, and the ugly.

   a. One idea is to provide a prize for the person or team who comes up with the most ideas.
   b. Groups can take allotted time to brainstorm solo and then as a group.

3. At the end, count the number of ideas and give the prize out.

4. As a team, review ideas and then build upon each other's ideas with "Yes and…"

5. Converge

   a. Give everyone the ability to vote for their favorites. Depending on the number of ideas, provide 3 to 5 votes each.
   b. Bucket the ideas with the most votes into themes and work together to find insights.

6. Summarize ideas and discuss which one to prototype. This can be a team decision or individual decision.[6]

Also, some examples of ways to use brainstorming for selecting technology include:

1. Brainstorm vendors. Take so much time to find different vendors to review.
2. Brainstorm ways technology can assist the team.
3. Brainstorm ways that technology can enhance candidate, recruiter, or hiring manager's experience.
4. Brainstorm the features needed in the technology.
5. Brainstorm the different ways the team can use the technology. For example, Video interviewing tools can also be used to create employee testimonial videos, reference checks, debrief a candidate or hiring manager, surveys, etc.

Amazing technology exists that can be incorporated in the talent acquisition strategy. Finding the right technology and the right vendor is critical. Design thinking can assist with ensuring the right tool is found for everyone in the process, and brainstorming is a great way to get lots of ideas from a team.

A brainstorming template is included at the end of the book as well as at *www.HireByDesignBook.com.*

Thus, technology can improve the experience of candidates, recruiters, hiring managers, and so forth. The next chapter is going to deal with the people experience and how to use empathy to create the best experience for everyone in the selection and hiring process.

## SEVEN

PEOPLE EXPERIENCE AND EMPATHY

Customer service, or the way companies interact with their customers, can make or break a company. Negative social media comments to negative reviews can altered a company's image. Everyone has a story about customer service. The story below contains one of my experiences.

While traveling on my 40th birthday vacation with a few friends, I had the worst customer service experience with an airline. Our digital boarding did not work, the Transportation Security Administration (TSA) agent and the airline agent showed no concern about our problem, and we ended up missing our flight. The gate agent must have been having a horrible day because there was zero customer service. It got to the point where I had to ask her to be nice to us because we were having a rough day. She then said, "Maybe I am having a bad day too." I had to point out that we were the customers.

This experience unfortunately never got any better. On our flight home, our boarding passes still did not work. Thankfully, I made sure to have both the app and hard copy passes this time. Funny thing, it was the hard copy boarding passes that did not work this time!

If I were telling you this story in person, I would be shouting off the rooftop about which airline this was. In fact, I could even tell you what group hires the agents, flight attendants, etc. for this company; because after this dreadful experience, I just had to check. Being in talent acquisition, people ask me all the time if I have any feedback about companies, so I need to make sure I have the information requested.

One negative experience can impact an airline by losing customers, potential employees, and sales. Therefore, attention to customer service issues is extremely important if a company wants to project a positive image.

Being empathetic with people is similarly necessary during selection process experiences. Individuals relate poor candidate experience just as much as poor customer service experience. My personal experience with people who are in their career search is that they focus on telling about the bad experiences. It almost becomes a snowball effect when candidates talk to other candidates and tell them about their experience with companies. Candidate resentment can ultimately impact a business' bottom line.

An effective resource for getting data about candidate experience is through The Talent Board, the first non-profit organization focused on the elevation and promotion of a quality candidate experience. The Talent Board awards companies with the highest positive candidate ratings with their CandE Awards every year.[1]

Here is a snapshot of the 2019 North American Talent Board Report:[2]

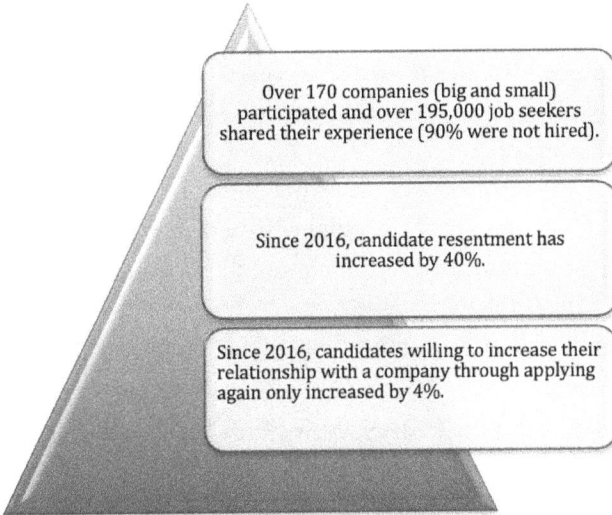

Over 170 companies (big and small) participated and over 195,000 job seekers shared their experience (90% were not hired).

Since 2016, candidate resentment has increased by 40%.

Since 2016, candidates willing to increase their relationship with a company through applying again only increased by 4%.

The above data generates the question, what can companies do to lower candidate resentment and increase a candidate's positive view and relationship with the company? Some approaches address the following:

- Feedback improves the experience. When given feedback, candidate willingness to increase their relationship with the employer goes up 20%.
- When a candidate is rejected, companies that provide general and specific feedback on qualifications and job fit resent rate decreases by 29%.
- During the screening and interviewing phase, when rejected candidates get specific job-related feedback, their overall "great experience" increases over 20%.
- Asking the candidate for feedback can increase candidate experience.

  - 72% increase when asked for research and application feedback
  - 148% increase when asked for screen/interview feedback
  - 76% increase when asked for feedback prior to starting

- Communication can improve the experience. Constant communication throughout the process has shown to increase the candidate's experience.

  - Rejection over phone – 29% higher experience than email message
  - Chatbot communication – 80% more likely to increase their relationship with employer
  - Text messages/notifications – 50% higher candidate experience[3]

Most companies focus on the candidate experience; however, a company needs to address issues other than just the candidate.

Who are the people in the selection process?

- Candidates
- Candidate's family or support group
- Talent Acquisition Team
- Human Resources Team
- Hiring Managers
- Interview Team
- Business Leaders

By focusing on the whole group, a company will ensure a more positive candidate experience, as well as employee experience. One bad apple ruins the bunch; therefore, an understanding of the importance of each group is presented.

Candidates

In the recruiting process, candidates need to experience what it feels like to work for the company. The company should treat candidates with respect and show them how amazing it would be for them to work with the company. In return, candidates will do the same thing. They want to highlight their fit for the role and why how they would be the best candidate. This relationship is similar to dating.

Candidate Family /Support Group

Most of the time companies never think about the family or support group. If the family and support groups are not considered, then the company is not truly paying attention to the person they are hiring. They will not know whether the candidate has a spouse, partner, children, dog, cat, parents, goldfish, etc. Questions emerge also: How will they be impacted if s/he takes this job? How much influence do they have? The support group of the candidate can make or break the offer.

Talent Acquisition Team

Since the talent acquisition team is the face of the company, the group needs to feel appreciated. Having disgruntled employees start the hiring process will lead to poor candidate experience and poor hiring.

Human Resources (HR) Team

The HR team is important because they are either the middleman between the talent acquisition team and business, or they are the talent acquisition team.

Hiring Manager

A streamline, efficient process will help in making knowledgeable decisions. Constant communication will ensure that the hiring manager is updated in the recruitment and selection process.

Interview Team

A company asks employees/staff to take time to be a part of the process, so these individuals need to get appreciation and feedback for their service. Additionally, the team needs to know what to look for and what information to provide.

Business Leaders

Leaders want new hires that will help them reach business goals. Keeping leaders informed helps show that the talent acquisition team is knowledgeable and responsible.

All the above groups touch recruiting in one way or another. A poor candidate experience can give negative press OR a company may lose the right candidate for the job, thus, negatively affecting the company's bottom line. The well-known phrase, "A Happy Wife is a Happy Life," reflects the status of the interview—if one of the support group does not like the company, job, or expectations, the interview might as well end immediately.

When it comes to hiring, the TA Team and HR Team are the sales team for the company. An inefficient sales team does not hit sales numbers. The Hiring Manager is one of the two "customers" for the TA/HR Team. If the hiring manager is not happy or does not feel like s/he is getting what s/he wants, it is not going to be productive for anyone. Does a company really want disgruntled employees a part of the interview process? Obviously, the answer is that they do not so the company needs to make sure the interview team is happy too. Also, everyone wants to make sure that the leaders of the business have what they need to ensure the company's success. There have been many instances where a company fails and affects everyone within that company.

In order to have a good "people experience" for those involved in the selection process, empathy is needed. The Merriam-Webster Dictionary's definition of empathy is

> the action of understanding, being aware of, being sensitive to, and vicariously experiencing the feelings, thoughts, and experience of another of either the past or present without having the feelings, thoughts and experience fully communicated in an objectively explicit manner.[4]

Within design thinking, empathy is used throughout the process. One goal of design thinking is to see another person's perspective. Design thinking has a one-step focus on empathy. It is the "Immersive Empathy" step. Emotional triggers motivate people, and sharing those triggers helps focus on a common goal. The goal of immersive empathy is to immerse oneself directly into a situation that evokes empathy. There are four different ways to accomplish this goal:

1. *Change Your Perspective.* What are some ways you can change your perspective to better relate to someone who has a different perspective?
2. *Limit Yourself.* How can you imagine having limited experience, much like your audience? What happens when you take that ability away from yourself?
3. *Do It Yourself.* How can you personally experience what your audience will experience? Have you tried it yourself? What does it feel like?
4. *Engage in an Analogous Experience.* Are there similar experiences in other industries that you can learn from?[5]

The first step is to plan what learnings will come from immersion of empathy in candidates, for example. First, it is important to find ways to get to know them. One way is to come up with answers to these questions.

1. How does it feel to apply to a position on the career site?
2. How does it feel to complete the pre-employment assessment?
3. How does it feel to receive no communication or feedback from an employer – aka being ghosted
4. How does it feel to ask questions to the chatbot?

The next step is to use the four ways to "immerse in empathy" above to brainstorm some ideas (5-10) for experiences that would help better understand the different perspectives. Below are examples for each way based on the questions above.

1. Change Your Perspective: Apply to a position on the career site

Example: In order to gain perspective of what a candidate is going through when applying, apply to other company websites to get a glimpse at what they are currently doing. Possibly start with competitors. These are companies that your candidates will be applying to as well.

2. Limit Yourself: Receive no communication or feedback from an employer – aka being ghosted

Example: You may think that you will not be able to experience ghosting to understand. To do this, ask your manager to ghost you when you least expect it. Your manager just needs to ignore your question. After not getting a response, have your manager meet with you so you can go through the emotions of not hearing back.

3. Do It Yourself: Complete the pre-employment assessment

Example: Has anyone on the team ever taken the pre-employment assessment? Have someone take and document their feelings throughout the assessment.

4. Engage in an Analogous Experience: Ask questions to the chatbot

Example: Chatbots are used for several different types of services and products. Go to a site and use the chatbot and document the experience.

Next, the hiring team should pick one of these and answer the following questions:

1. What will you do?
2. How will you do it?
3. What props or tools do you need? and
4. Whose help will you need?

Now, it is time to conduct the empathy experience and note feelings, learnings, and any surprises. Reflecting and writing down what has changed or what was uncovered will be included in moving forward. This is all about finding a new point of view.

Being in the business of recruiting, talent acquisition professionals can be numb to a lot of the experiences a candidate goes through. They forget the feeling of losing a job or looking for a job. Also, if this is the first time to hire, there is uncertainty in the process. Immersive empathy is a great way to be able to understand completely the perspective of someone else in the selection process.

People experience and communication go hand in hand. Our next chapter will dive deeper into communication and how to use extremes to identify insights.

## EIGHT

COMMUNICATION FOR THE EXTREMES

Lack of communication is one of the areas that candidates complain the most about in the hiring process. For a candidate, looking for a new job can be stressful; and when communication is lacking, it makes the process harder. This can happen to anyone. Here is an example from when I was looking for a job after graduation.

After I graduated from the University of Evansville in December of 2001, I moved back home to find my first job after college. Graduating after 9/11, there were not a lot of positions for recent graduates. It took me about six months to land my first "real" job. During my career search, I created a way to stay organized with all the roles that I applied to and would document my status for each.

At a job fair, I met with a company that was close to where I lived at the time. They had a role in Human Resources and the hours were 11AM – 7PM. At the time, I loved those hours and I applied to the company. I never received any feedback or decision, so I assumed I was not selected. About six months later, I received a letter in the mail notifying me that I was not selected for the role. Let me say it again – six months later! I might have been young, but I was not stupid. I knew within weeks I did not get the job. That put a bad taste in my mouth for this company. I have told this story several times since and have included the company name when speaking to friends.

Everyone probably has some sort of story similar to this. Ghosting, where a person or company does not respond or communicate during the hiring process, has been a hot topic lately. Companies have been ghosting candidates for a long time; however, recently candidates have begun ghosting companies. In fact, it has become quite common. So, if companies can ghost candidates, then there is no reason candidates cannot ghost companies.

Communication equals respect. Therefore, candidates need to be communicated with in a timely fashion, which, in turn, will limit risks for the company. Understanding the type of communication needed during the process is the first step.

There at least 26 different times to communicate during the selection process. Communication can be with candidates, hiring manager, interviewing team, etc. Here is list of those communications and to whom.

Candidate	Hiring Manager/Business
Acknowledgement of receipt of application	Confirm job posting, interview process
Request information from candidate	Availability for interviews
Respond to company information	Candidate review
Status updates	Confirmation of interview
Pre-employment assessment	Evaluation/Feedback from interview
Availability for interviews	Obtain Offer Approval/Comp approval
Confirmation of interview	Offer accepted or declined
Obtain feedback from interview	Confirm start date
Pre-close candidate for offer	Status report or update of job requisition
Offer extended	Request feedback on process
Background check/reference check	
Confirm start date	
Welcome new hire and first day details	
Letter of no interest to the unqualified applicants	
Notify position is filled, cancelled or on hold	
Request feedback on process	

Who is responsible for communicating?

Most of the communication to the candidate will be through the Human Resources/Talent Acquisition team. This gives the candidate one point of contact. However, the hiring manager needs to be communicating with the Human Resources/Talent Acquisition team to ensure the process is more streamline.

Tools to use

Setting expectations on how to communicate and with whom will give the candidate a better experience. Communication preferences should be identified immediately. The team, with candidate's input, needs to clarify the mode of communication: email, text, or phone call. This is important because if a candidate does not know the preferred method of communication, s/he will undoubtedly waste everyone's time and use all communication tools to communicate the same thing. A voicemail message that states when voicemails will be returned will help alleviate those frequent calls from a candidate. If this is the process, the calls must be returned at the time stated on the voicemail.

Some communication can be automated to make it easier on the hiring team. Also, there are pieces of communication that a chatbot can respond to as well. Here are the communications that can be automated or use chatbots:

Confirm application received

Answer simple FAQs about the company

Schedule interviews

Send Pre-employment Assessment email

Confirm interview

Offer accepted/declined to hiring manager

Confirm start date

Welcome onboarding info

Obtain feedback on process

A lot of companies would add the following two:

Letter of no interest

Notify position is filled, cancelled, or on hold

Automation may be fine to use sometimes with these two. However, one of the main complaints from candidates is that they receive no feedback. They want to know what they could have done differently or what experience/skills they are lacking for the job. Companies are typically concerned about risk at this point. Will the candidate sue or take the information and use it against the company in some way? There has to be a way to provide feedback to candidates with little or no risk; but that means there must be a good reason why s/he is not getting the role.

Automated emails are typically cold and lack any personal feel. Creating a personalized email will show a candidate that the company cares about the candidate. A phone call is even better. If a role is filled, cancelled, or put on hold and the candidate is someone to consider in the future, being more personal may keep that candidate interested in the company.

After talking to many job seekers and hearing their issues with communication in the hiring process, I decided to conduct a Case Study that focuses on Communication in the Hiring Process. Design thinking will be the methodology for this study. The goal was to have this case study completed this year. Given the restrictions of the pandemic of 2020, completion of the total process was unattainable. However, the following information provides the major components of that study.

The first step is to come up with my challenge statement and description.

My Challenge Statement

How might we design a communication plan for the hiring process that ensures constant communication with feedback to people and limits any risk for the company?

Description:

A career search can be stressful and exciting at the same time. The goal is to find the best position that matches the person's interest, skill, experience, and work environment. Companies are looking to fill role(s) that are needed for the success of the business. The hiring process should be thorough for both the person and company. Communication between people and companies needs to be consistent and honest. What people typically get is limited, random, or no communication (aka black hole). At this point, people are happy with the bare minimum; and even the yes or no automation emails will suffice. This is not the ideal experience for the person nor will it help the company's employer reputation. Companies are super busy or have limited people power to communicate to all people who apply, interview, etc., especially people who are not moving forward. Finding a way that makes sense can be hard. Also, companies are afraid to provide feedback and possibly get sued. The risk outweighs the need to communicate feedback. Due to this inconsistent communication, ghosting is happening on both sides – for companies and for people. How can the company find a solution that gives people information to help them understand the process and get feedback to help them with their career search? How can companies create a communication process that is effective and efficient plus having it provide feedback with limited risk?

From there I created a list of observation ideas, including whom I would observe, where I would observe, and what I would look for in my observation.

Observation Ideas:

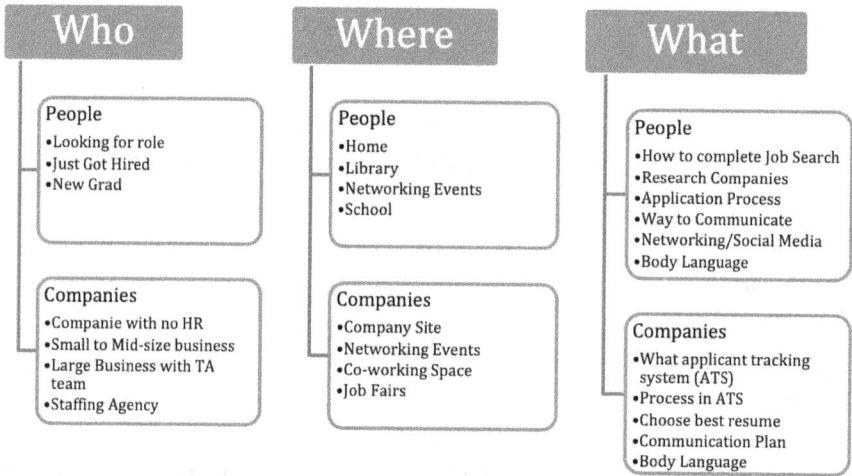

Who	Where	What
People	**People**	**People**
•Looking for role	•Home	•How to complete Job Search
•Just Got Hired	•Library	•Research Companies
•New Grad	•Networking Events	•Application Process
	•School	•Way to Communicate
		•Networking/Social Media
		•Body Language
Companies	**Companies**	**Companies**
•Companie with no HR	•Company Site	•What applicant tracking system (ATS)
•Small to Mid-size business	•Networking Events	•Process in ATS
•Large Business with TA team	•Co-working Space	•Choose best resume
•Staffing Agency	•Job Fairs	•Communication Plan
		•Body Language

The next steps include: observe both candidates and companies, interview both of them, review all notes, and cluster insights into themes. From there, the final steps are ideation, prototyping, and the recommendation for this challenge. The final case study will be available at *www.hiringblueprint.co.*

Another case study focusing on feedback for candidates is a case study through The Talent Board. They looked at PointClickCare and what efforts they have been making to provide feedback to candidates.

PointClickCare is a long term and post-acute care provider. When looking at feedback for candidates, they started with what the candidates call the "black hole," which means that after a candidate applies, nothing happens. Their application goes into the black hole of nothingness.

The "black hole" is the applicant tracking system! PointClickCare implemented a new ATS which helped with this challenge. They were able to automate parts of the recruitment workflow which allowed their recruiters to focus on more important matters – the candidates. The new ATS provides customized email templates that integrate with Outlook, so candidates can receive status updates and are kept in the loop.

By implementing these changes, PointClickCare has seen an improvement with their Glassdoor interview ratings. By finding the best ways to automate workflow and giving the recruiters easy to use tools, PointClickCare was able to improve their communication with candidates which, in turn, improved their candidate experience.[1]

Talent Acquisition professionals have had stalkers and silent bombs. Stalkers are the candidates who call, text, and email multiple times a day. They are desperate to get a status. Talent acquisition professionals know their name and their phone number by heart. Then, there are the candidates who never communicate and are always unavailable when attempting to contact them. It is at this point that the talent acquisition professional becomes the stalker. Silent bombs are the candidates who do not respond to calls, emails, or text. These are typically the candidates the hiring manager wants to interview.

Obviously, these are the extremes of candidate behavior. Not all candidates call, text, or email daily; and not all candidates ghost. Wouldn't it be nice to know exactly how to communicate with these extremes? Or what process or solution can work with both the stalker and the bombs?

Identifying Extremes with Candidate Communication

When using design thinking to solve a problem, understanding the extremes can help stretch thinking and look beyond assumptions to get new ideas. The first step is to identify the extremes.

An extreme audience is the group of people who either have no experience or a lot of experience, whereas the mainstream is right in the middle with experience. The range of an audience can look like a bell-shaped curve. The extremes are at both ends and the mainstream is in the middle where the curve is the highest.

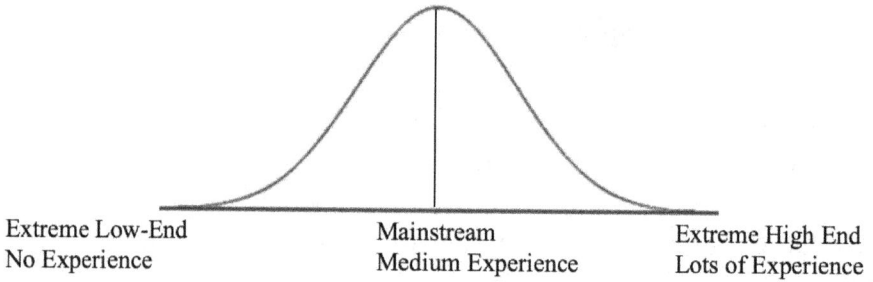

| Extreme Low-End | Mainstream | Extreme High End |
| No Experience | Medium Experience | Lots of Experience |

One extreme is no professional experience, and the other extreme is 20+ years of professional experience.

Step One: What lenses can be used to find extremes?

The lenses could be demographics, behaviors, or motivations. Some other ways to look at this would be through expertise, attitude, life stage, familiarity of company, social media behaviors, etc.

Step Two: Using the lenses, how they be stretched to identify specific people/behaviors?

Come up with 5 to 8 examples of the extremes. These are the people creating the learnings and may be observing or interviewing. Be as specific as possible. Select a couple and figure out the areas of curiosity and areas to learn about them.

Here is an example:

. . .

Challenge statement: How do we communicate the steps of the interview process in an easy to use and find manner for entry-level position?

For the no experience extreme:

- A candidate with a high school diploma or equivalent with no working experience
- A candidate with 1 to 2 years of experience in retail or fast food restaurant
- A new graduate from college with work study experience only

For with experience extreme:

- A candidate who has retired from his or her career of 30+ years of experience and looking for an entry-level role to make additional money in retirement
- A candidate who is looking for a new career opportunity in a new industry with 15 years of experience in a different industry
- A candidate who has several years of experience in the same entry-level role for a different company

With these extremes, it is time to build questions to use for the interview.

Some example questions:

- When researching a company, what sites do you go to?
- When applying to a position, when do you typically learn about the steps of the interview and hiring process?

  - When do you want this information?
  - How would you want this information provided to you?

- What is your primary communication tool?
- How would you prefer to communicate with a company?

These are questions that need to be included in interviews with the extreme and mainstream groups. The learnings from the extreme groups will help with the mainstream group. Typically, finding a solution for the extremes, the solution works for the people in the middle too.

Constant and relevant communication is needed in the selection process. Having a framework, easy to use templates, and tools, the hiring teams will be able to communicate more. Extremes in design thinking will provide a way to think outside the box and help the team come up with ideas for both the extremes and middle too.

All these potential changes and improvements to the selection process create excitement about analytics and measuring success. In the next chapter, the discussion will be about analytics for measuring performance with the talent acquisition strategy.

## NINE

ANALYTICS WITH PROTOTYPING

Being able to measure the performance of a business is paramount. Company teams and technology help understand successes, areas of improvement, and return on investment. Creating the right analytics using big data can provide a nice dashboard or scorecard on performance.

While at a large fortune 500 company, the business leaders did not understand what my team did. They assumed that it did not take a lot to hire. Generally speaking, most leaders do not understand the whole process of hiring. Typically, the hiring manager comes in two-thirds of the way into the process. If there were not clearly outlined procedures for hiring in a manual somewhere, it would be understandable why business leaders would not know what a talent acquisition team does. I decided to make sure that my team, my manager, and my clients – business leaders – understood all the effort it took for my team to hire.

To do this, I first ensured that all hiring managers understood our selection process. We created an interview training that each recruiter conducted and had all managers attend. This provided them with an understanding of the process, what to do and not do during the interview, and how to build a relationship with the recruiter.

Understanding the process is great, but that does not show the effort it takes to hire. So next, we had to create reports that provided data around hiring. Reports that covered key metrics and hiring results needed to be created monthly, quarterly, and yearly.

To determine key metrics, we needed a scorecard for the talent acquisition team to track performance. Having a scorecard that the business leaders would understand helped ensure that they would review it and understand it. The scorecard could help the talent acquisition team track trends with their numbers and performance. The scorecard had specific metrics that focused on survey results from new hires and hiring managers. It was all in one place for them to review. The scorecard could be presented to the business leaders, as well as to the Human Resource or Talent Acquisition Leader on the team's performance.

Metrics for a scorecard need to be based on the talent acquisition strategy and goals. Based on the Talent Acquisition team member, some of the metrics were different for each team member based on the type of hiring roles or the business location, etc. It was not a one size fits all scorecard. One location may have more cows than people so the candidate pool was smaller. Another location could be in a city where there are tons of candidates but have a hard time getting offer acceptance. And then another team member recruits for roles that are hard to fill—or what talent acquisition industry call purple squirrels. What stays consistent is the data and the metrics provided to the business leaders to show performance and results.

There are so many possible recruiting metrics out there to use and understanding these will help with measuring performance goals for the team or company. There are different ways to measure performance throughout the process. Recruiting metrics can be placed in five categories:

Recruitment Marketing

Recruitment Marketing metrics focus on measuring the Recruitment Marketing Strategy, including Employer Brand, Social Media, Career Site, and Candidate Experience.

Speed of Hiring

Speed of hiring metrics focus on measuring the amount of time it takes to hire. This can include the amount of time between each step to the time to fill.

Quality of Hiring

Quality of Hiring metrics focus on measuring the quality of the hire. This can include metrics on the new hire's performance, tenure, or engagement.

Expense of Hiring

Expense of hiring metrics focus on the cost to hire. This includes the cost to attract to onboard.

Source of Hiring

Source of hiring metrics focus on measuring the different ways of finding a candidate. This includes external resources, like job boards to internal resources like employee referral program.

Metrics should measure quality—quality of the candidate to the quality of the hire. Here are 12 metrics to focus on.

1. *Net Promoter Score* – How likely are potential candidates or employees to recommend the company as a great place to work?

The net promoter score will provide a look into the employer brand, employee value proposition, and employee engagement. Using the net promoter score throughout the process can help determine if there are any areas of concern in different steps of the selection process, onboarding, and work environment.

2. *Satisfaction* – How satisfied are the candidates, new hires, and stakeholders with overall selection and hiring process?

Another great metric to use throughout the process is feedback from the candidates, new hires, and stake holders (hiring managers, trainers, human resources, and business leaders). Surveys can be sent throughout the selection process. Once the position is filled, the hiring manager can be asked to complete a quick survey for that specific role and the process. There are some easy ways to automate this process through an applicant tracking system or human resources information system.

3. *Conversion rates* – What percentage of people complete a specific action?

There are several places that one can look at conversion rates. These rates help the team understand the audience and where there may be a bottleneck in the process.

- *Career Site/Landing Page*

  The career site/landing page reveals how many people apply, join the talent pool, register for an event or ask a question, etc. This shows that the site is targeting the right audience and providing the right content.

- *Application Form*

  If someone clicks to apply, the goal is a completed application. This also shows if the right candidates are being targeted and if the application process is easy to use.

- *Email Campaign*

Email campaigns should be targeted to the ideal candidate. This shows how many read and completed the task requested in the email. That task could be to apply to a role, register for an event, read the blog, etc.

- *Social Media*

Similar to the email campaign, social media needs to target ideal candidates. Understanding the conversation rate will show what social media channel should be focused on and what content the ideal candidate wants.

4. *Engagement* – How engaged are people during the process?

Keeping people engaged is important to any experience. Getting people to follow the company page, to ask questions, and to share the company's message demonstrates engagement. Likewise, companies want people to follow their company, ask questions, and share their message. This can be on the career site or landing page, social media, and company page.

New hire engagement is important as well. The new hires should be brand ambassadors for the business as well as hiring.

5. *Career Site Traffic* – How effective are the approaches to attract people to the career site?

With a career site, there are different ways to attract people. Those include:

1. *Paid advertising campaigns* through different channels like LinkedIn, Google Adwords, etc.
2. *Organic Searches* – finding the company through a search engine
3. *Keywords* – words or phrases that bring people to the site.

Track the sources that bring the most traffic to the career site. This gives a good understanding of where to use money for any paid channels.

6. Retention / Turnover Rate – What is the percentage of employees that stay or leave the company in a certain period of time?

Retention and turnover rates can help with determining quality of hire. The main question is when does turnover fall under hiring? Some companies will say within the first six months or year. My recommendation is to only look at turnover in the first month when correlating it with hiring.

7. Qualified Candidates and Hires – What channels are producing qualified candidates and hires for the company?

This is a great metric to focus on quality in the talent acquisition strategy. Not all qualified candidates will be hired. An easy way to determine a quality candidate is by seeing if any candidate moves forward from the first step. Again, ensuring that the talent acquisition strategy is targeting the qualified candidates in the right places includes the following:

- *Source* – job boards, programmatic advertising, social media, referrals, etc...
- *Employee Referral Program* – employees providing qualified candidates and if not, strategy for improvement
- *External Referrals* – customers, fans, former employees, etc. who refer candidates. Who are the most productive in finding quality candidates?

8. Ramp Up Time – time required for a new hire to hit full productivity

There are ways to determine the quality of a hire: the amount of time it takes new hires to get up and running; and given a structured training program, the time it takes for them to be at 100% performance after completing training. This will look different for each role and each company.

9. Cost

Budget is important for any business. How much is a business willing to spend on finding a new hire? This will be different for every organization, as well as for the different roles. Coming up with a structured calculation cost will keep this consistent. Cost can include marketing costs to recruiter's salary to hiring manager's time to onboard.

- *Cost per qualified applicant* – This includes the cost to source and advertise. Calculate this by position to a time frame.
- *Cost per hire* – The total amount of money spent to hire a candidate.
- *Cost to fill* – This may sound like the same as cost per hire but it is not. This does not include the cost of anything prior to the candidate getting into the pipeline. This is the cost to fill based on the candidate pool.

10. *Time in stage* – This is the time it takes a candidate to complete each stage or step in the selection process from application to start date

Ratios are my favorite metric for recruiter performance. Here are the different ratios:

- Applicant to Hire Ratio
- Test to Hire Ratio
- Hiring Manager Interview to Offer Ratio
- Hiring Manager Interview to Hire Ratio
- Offer to Hire Ratio

My former team hired call center agents monthly. They used these ratios to understand the number of applicants, completed tests, hiring manager interviews, and offers for future classes. This metric showed new hires how they were improving throughout the years. It also provided information on trends during the year, when there was a higher probability to hire more, and months where there were the lowest number of candidates. All of this aided in creating a more efficient way to perform our jobs.

11. *Offer acceptance rate* – How many candidates accepted the offer?

This metric can show quality in a couple of different ways. It can show the quality of the selection process and strategy. It can show the quality of the hiring manager's interview skills, as well as the overall quality of hires. The goal is to be as close to 100% as possible and not to have declined offers. Typically, declined offers means the selection process will have to be repeated.

12. *Time to source, find, and hire*

- *Time to source* – days it takes to source a qualified candidate
- *Time to find* – days it takes to have a qualified candidate apply
- *Time to hire* – time it takes to complete the selection process

Hiring managers typically want a new hire to start immediately. The amount of time to find and source candidates to hire is an important metric to hiring managers. It is also important to the talent acquisition team because the cost of hire can go up and satisfaction can go down. However, this should not be the number one metric for the talent acquisition team. If it is, the quality of the hires will probably go down and engagement of the team will go down.

To use these metrics, the data has to be tracked. Working with the analytics team or the recruitment partners/vendors can help establish the metrics and reporting. Reporting should be easy to understand and suitable for the audience.

Creating a prototype for reporting or analytics dashboard is a fast way to get feedback and build the best solution for the company and the target audience. A prototype brings an idea to life. It makes it tangible and shareable. Prototypes give the ability to work out the kinks and get feedback before spending a lot of money on the final product/solution. During this time, edits and mistakes can be corrected in an inexpensive way.

When looking at how to create a dashboard of metrics to deliver to the business, there are two different prototypes.

1. *Digital prototype:* Digital prototypes help work out how the dashboard will be engaging experience –use paper, cardboard, people, and video recording to do that. No programming is needed.

2. *Experience prototype:* This involves creation of an experience – this can be how to present the metrics (charts, deck, or actual presentation). Storyboards may be a good method to use with the experience prototype.

Here is an example of a prototype that was created for the library to attract more children and encourage reading during one of my IDEO U classes. This is a prototype app.

There is a chance that any prototype may be scrapped and may require starting over so one should not get too attached to the prototype. It is fine to be excited, but there must also be a willingness to change if that is best for the project.

When sharing, it is acceptable to paint the picture of how the prototype is going to work but do not sell the prototype. Also, feedback from the audience is most important, so everyone on the team should pay attention to the person giving feedback, take notes, and listen with eyes and ears. Then, the team can take that information and go back to the drawing board to improve the prototype. This may need to be done several times before the final prototype.

Using a prototype to create a reporting tool or analytic dashboard will provide the data and the look and feel the target audience wants. It gives the ability to get their feedback up front so that providing this data is exactly what they want to see. If what the audience is looking for is not what is presented, then the process can take additional time to create and leaves the audience hanging.

At the end of the book and at *www.HireByDesignBook.com,* there is a Scorecard template.

Being able to measure the quality of the hire helps ensure that the right talent for the organization is being chosen. After hiring top performers, the next step is to retain them. Design thinking gives ways to understand top performers and ensure that they stay with the business. This discussion will take place in our next chapter.

## TEN

RETENTION OF TOP PERFORMERS USING OBSERVATION AND INTERVIEWING

The more time, money, and energy it takes to hire candidates, the more a business wants to retain them. If the talent acquisition strategy is linked to the business strategy, every hire will impact the business. Losing one can jeopardize the performance of the business. Therefore, it is important to have a strategy on retaining performers.

One of my favorite resources is the *Harvard Business Review.* The magazine contains many topics and case studies for readers to review and gather new insights. One of these articles, viewed over five million times on the web, was written by Patty McCord and highlighted a Netflix PowerPoint deck about talent management ideas.

The Netflix presentation by Reed Hastings (former CEO) and Patty McCord (former Chief Talent Officer) focused on "how they shaped the culture and motivated performance at Netflix." *Harvard Business Review,* January-February 2014. Their approach was all about common sense.

In 2001 and 2002, Patty realized two important pieces of talent management. One is that a company must hire A players. "A players" are the people that fit the specific business strategy and are strong performers. The second is that the team must evolve with the company. A business cannot retain employees who no longer meet the expectations or changes of the business. This means business leaders have to be willing to let employees go who no longer have the skills needed to move forward. Employees need to be rewarded for what they were able to accomplish while at the company (aka sweet severance package).

When looking at how to manage their employees, Netflix does not rely on formal policies. They rely on logic and common sense; and because of this, they have seen better results and lower costs. They try to hire people who are focused on the company's interest. Netflix saw that 97% of their hires would last more than more 3 years. They noticed that the other 3% of their hires would last less than a year. Would it make sense for them to write policies for just 3% of their hires? Therefore, their goal is not to hire the 3% category; but if they did, they let them go as soon as they realized they had made a mistake.

Netflix also asks managers to have performance conversations throughout the year. They do not have a yearly performance review or performance improvement plans. They focus on honest communication and focus on what the company needs from their employees. If an employee does not have the skills needed for where the company is going, they let the person go with a nice severance package. Netflix uses a 360-degree review that is simple and helps them identify areas they should stop, start, or continue.

Most companies would say that HR or Talent Acquisition owns hiring and company culture; but at Netflix, their managers own the recruiting and leaders' own culture. Human Resources is a part of the business team and need to be just as innovative as other parts of the company.

Netflix decided not to mimic other companies or just stick to the standard normal with their talent management. They focused on who they are, what they wanted out of the employees, and what they wanted for their employees. Understanding their employee helped them build the right talent management strategy and work culture.[1]

Some business leaders may be thinking, "Netflix is a well-known brand, and everyone is running to work there. My company is not well known, or my industry has high turnover so we can never be like Netflix."

Following is a personal example of how my former employer retained top talent.

I have worked for a company where most people have a negative taste in their mouth about the company because of what they do; namely, student loans and collections. There were times at job fairs when people would literally run away from me when I told them where I worked; or they would start complaining to me about their loan or asking me questions on how to do something with their loan. Obviously, talent acquisition teams know nothing about loans or the system, and they cannot erase a loan from the system.

To get people excited about working for the company, the talent acquisition team talks about our work environment and promotion opportunities. Most of my time there, approximately 95% to 100% of our leaders were promoted from within. At one point, our site leader started at the company as a collector at a different office. We were proud of our ability to promote from within. That was something that differentiated us from our competitors, and it helped us retain our top talent.

Another example is Hyatt Hotels. The hospitality industry is known for having high turnover, but here is an example of how Hyatt focused on retaining its top employees.

Based on an article on Snacknation, the hospitality industry turnover is estimated to be at 73.8% annual rate. Hyatt Hotels has been able to keep their turnover rate well below that of the industry's average. Hyatt has made retention initiatives central to their business initiatives. Some of these initiatives involve an in-depth training program, a Caring Fund for employees facing emergency situations, and diversity and inclusion initiatives.

Hyatt empowers their employees with training and development initiatives and treats them like family. Their focus on people is at the heart of their business. Hyatt provides a safe, secure, and empowering environment for their employees. Focusing on the person enables Hyatt to create the work environment and culture to retain their employees.[2]

When looking at retention, most companies do not understand who owns retention. Companies continue to throw retention at different parts of the company--from Human Resources to front line supervisors to the CEO. Retention is owned by everyone in the company. Executives, Human Resources, Front Line Managers, and even employees should care about retention. Human Resources and the analytics team can measure and track retention, but it should not just fall on Human Resources.

My personal experience as a manager is that retention is a serious issue. It takes a lot of time to train and develop a talent acquisition team. In selecting the team, the goal is to ensure that they will stay with the company and remain top performers. In the same way, my manager, my clients (Hiring Managers), our candidates, and employees also need to care that the team stays with the company.

Executives should care about retention as well. Leaders and managers need to know their team's worth. Executives must answer the question: If a whole team gives notice at the same time, how will that impact the business? Can the business carry on or will there be a snag or bottle neck where the company may lose business, money, or time, etc. By answering these questions, leaders, management, internal clients, and the team will understand the worth of the team.

There are also times where there is a need for a team member to leave the team – either for a new role in the company or leave the company for another opportunity. And that is ok. There is such a thing as healthy turnover and it should happen.

When should a business keep someone or let them go?

There are several reasons for healthy turnover: performance, work ethic viola-
tion, team dynamics issues, the person has outgrown the role, the person can
do more for the company in a different role, or a lack of excitement or desire
for the position. When letting someone go, managers may feel like they
failed. It is acceptable to fail in hiring. Failure could mean that something
went wrong during the hiring process. Going back and understanding what
went wrong will provide information that will help with the future hiring
process. No one is perfect. When there is a failure, the goal is to learn
from it.

If one apple in a bunch is bad, what happens to the other apples? They go
bad too. Maintaining one under performer or "Negative Nancy" can jeopardize the whole team. No one is worth ruining team dynamics. But sometimes managers say, "I did not know that s/he was negative or bringing the
team down." If that manager's team heard this, they would roll their eyes.

Observing and Interviewing

By using observing and interviewing through design thinking, insights can
be gained about a team, the team's dynamics, and the assistance necessary for
the team to be successful.

Observing and interviewing are two ways to gain insight from employees,
team, clients, etc. Observation is better than focus groups because observation takes place in their natural state. When observing, the leader takes time
to sit with the team, sees what they do every day, listens to their conversations, and takes notes. It is important to just sit and watch and not ask questions. This can be the hardest part. If the team is in a cubicle environment,
the leader just grabs a cube, sits there, and works, while quietly observing.
Obviously, just staring at them could make them all feel uncomfortable. So,
the leader should be incognito; and if this is a problem, ask a peer to do it.
However, it is not a good idea to ask Human Resources, because employees
freak out when Human Resources is around.

After observing and taking notes, it is time to build interview questions. This
needs to be conducted through one on one meetings. Group discussions can

be a different experience for introverts and extraverts. Introverts will sit there freaking out, thinking that they may be called upon while extraverts often take over the meeting. Not all opinions will be heard. When scheduling the meeting, the leader should explain what the meeting is about and provide the questions up front. This gives everyone time to prepare for the conversation. The persons being interviewed should be informed that this is not going to hinder their employment or cause any negativity. All is confidential. If anything needs to be escalated, they will know it is happening. This is for the good of the team. There may be different questions for different team members based on the observations. For example, one team member may do a shortcut in the system and understanding why may be one of the questions. Another team member listens to music during work so there may be a question about the type of music they enjoy.

Most of the questions will focus on what they like and dislike about the team, what could the team do to be more productive, or any ideas to help the team be more successful. Is there anything that causes issues or delays? It is important to ask what they want from you as a manager, what they want from the company, and why they would stay or leave the organization. During the interview, questions should be asked about future career goals. This is an interview to gather as much information as possible so that everyone's answers are collected, reviewed, and clustered by themes. Gather insights from these and provide the insights to the team, leadership, and Human Resources to improve the work environment and retain employees.

Talent strategy and business strategy go hand and hand. Understanding what to look for in new hires and what employees want from the company will increase the ability to hire and retain the right talent for the organization.

Observation and Interviewing templates can be found at the end of the book and at *www.HireByDesignBook.com*.

Throughout this book we discussed different parts of the talent acquisition strategy and the different pieces of design thinking. Now it is time to put it all together and figure out what the next steps will be. The final chapter is all about the next steps and using iteration.

## ELEVEN

NEXT STEPS AND ITERATION

"Everyone who's ever taken a shower has an idea. It's the person who gets out of the shower, dries off and does something about it who makes a difference,"
~Nolan Bushnell[1]

About 15 years ago, a group of friends and I discussed a matchmaking site. We had all these great ideas on what the site would do and how it would match people. We even discussed a name for the site. We swore it would be a huge success and make us all a lot of money. We talked about this idea for years. In fact, I had a conversation about this idea with my husband recently. Did we do anything with this idea? No, we did not. Now, I am sure there is a site already out there that is similar to our idea.

My question to the reader is have you ever had a great idea and sat on it and, then, that same idea shows up online but created by someone else? Until someone acts on an idea, it is not innovation. Throughout this book, there are discussions about all the different steps of design thinking from coming up with ideas to prototyping. Now, it is time to talk about how to move the prototype into the solution.

After finalizing the prototype, the next step in the process is to share it with others and gather feedback. This includes sharing the prototype with individuals who will be using it, as well as people who are not going to use it. By getting feedback early, the prototype can be updated or even scrapped. In design thinking, the goal is to fail early so that success can come sooner. Risk is managed through iteration.

Iteration is continuing to update, enhance, and build prototypes until there is a confident design. Once this happens, it is time to pitch the prototype and, hopefully, start implementing it.

Here are the steps to iterate:

1. *Develop questions for Iteration* – look at the three lenses of design thinking and figure out what questions there are about the prototype. Come up with 6 to 9 questions.

> a. *Desirability:* figure out the desires of the person and create a solution that addresses the need and value
> b. *Feasibility:* determine if the solution is feasible
> c. *Viability:* ask if it makes business sense

2. *Rank the questions by importance* – What is the level of urgency and dependency? Which ones need to be looked at right away? Which ones are more critical? Which one should be asked first?

3. *Grab a few people and ask the questions* – Now, take the feedback and information obtained through the questions and diverge again. The goal is to learn and move forward.

4. *Take the information and conduct another ideation session* and determine if updating the current prototype or creating a new prototype is needed.

5. *Keep doing this until the prototype is ready* to be move forward to the pitch.

If a pitch is needed to sell the idea, the following need to be available:

1. *Current Situation* – What is it like now without the solution?
2. *Recent learnings* – What are the learnings and testing completed so far?
3. *Future Opportunity* – How will this improve the current situation? What questions were answered? Why is it valuable?
4. *Resources* – In order to make this come to life, what is needed (people, budget, time, and resources)?

The pitch needs to be concise, creative, and compelling. A great way to do this is with a storyboard. The presenter tells the story before and after the prototype. The goal of the pitch is to get approval to move forward to creating or implementing the solution. If there are questions or concerns, it is necessary to go back to iteration. Depending on the challenge statement and the solution, this process can be as fast as a few days or it could take months to complete.

Using design thinking needs to be a common practice. The world is always evolving and so should teams, businesses, etc. Everyone should take the time to review processes and gather feedback to see where there are opportunities to improve a process. Also, they should measure changes to see if there is a return on investment. Finally, they should show how utilizing design thinking is improving their business and their hiring.

What is so amazing about design thinking is that it can be part of different areas of business. This book is focused on hiring; but design thinking can be used in sales, accounting, operations, etc. if one takes the time to learn design thinking and then uses the methodology to find solutions in the respective business. Therefore, if a business has people involved (which all do!), then this should be a helpful tool.

The world is currently evolving with the coronavirus pandemic. The country went from having the lowest unemployment rate to the highest within four weeks. The only thing constant is change. When a business gets disrupted, it is time to step back and review the current strategies. As with the recession in 2007, all business entities will learn from the 2020 Covid-19 pandemic. They will take the opportunity to gather insights and find solutions that will help their business thrive in all economic climates.

From the time this book was first imagined to its actual writing, the world has changed. Our individual lives have changed from being out and about, shaking hands, and pushing through any illness without worry to sheltering in place, working from home, using social distancing, and encouraging our employees to stay home when they are sick. Our responses have been successful, such as learning to work from home and making very hard decisions on which jobs are essential to non-essential. By the time the book is published, everything will have changed again.

Change can make businesses grow or shrink. Taking design thinking principles and focusing on products, services, and experiences that are desirable, feasible, and viable will keep businesses moving forward. Also, taking the time to observe and interview other business leaders will provide knowledge about their business operations and, thus, provide more insight into best practices in the field. Employees' input is also important because they are the feet on the ground, they are the all-knowing of the customers, and they are the eyes and ears. Finally, leaders should give their teams the ability to take these design thinking principles to improve the business, services, and products.

My final words to the reader is that you must always want your business strategy and talent acquisition strategy to go hand in hand. The selection process is all about the people who are in the process. Ensure that the process is easy to use and provides the hiring team with the right amount of information to make good hiring decisions.

Growing up in the late '80s and '90s, there is one public service announcement that I have always remembered…. "The More You Know…"

The more you know about your business, your finances, and your people, the more you will grow.

TEMPLATES

Chapter 3:

- Talent Acquisition Strategy Template
- Sourcing Strategy Template
- Challenge Statement Template

Chapter 4:

- Candidate Persona Template
- Job Posting Template

Chapter 5:

- Onboarding Checklist
- Mash Up Session Template

Chapter 6:

- Brainstorming Template

Chapter 9:

- Recruiter Score Card Template

Chapter 10:

- Observation Template
- Interviewing Template

Talent Acquisition Strategy Template

Company Mission:	
TA Mission:	
Company Vision:	
TA Vision:	
Company Goals:	
TA Goals:	

Workforce Planning:	**Forecasting:**	**Turnover Rate:**

Employer Branding:	
Employee Value Proposition:	

Candidate Persona(s)	**Persona #1**	**Persona #2**	**Persona #3**
Sourcing Strategy by Persona:	**Persona #1**	**Persona #2**	**Persona #3**
Recruitment Marketing:	**Persona #1**	**Persona #2**	**Persona #3**

Online Strategy:	**Post Position:**	**Source Candidates:**

College Strategy:	
Grassroots Strategy:	

Selection Process:	
Evaluation Process:	
Onboarding Process:	

Key Performance Indicators:	**Reporting Analytics:**

Sourcing Strategy Template

Candidate Funnel	Time Frame	KPIs	Goals
Target Start Date:		# of Candidates	
Target Offer Date:		# of Phone Screens	
Interview:		# of Interviews	
Phone Screen:		# of Offers	
Resume Review:		# of Hires	
Target Job Posting Date:		Time to Fill	
Approval to Post Date:			

Online Recruitment:	College Recruitment:	Grass Roots Recruitment:
Job Boards	College Website Job Postings	Employee Referral Program
Social Media	On-site Interviews	Open House/Interview Day
Sourcing Tools	Meeting with Career Services/Professors	Radio
Networking Websites	Networking On-site	Billboard
Targeted Advertising	Presentations	Print
Banner Advertising	Job Fairs	Press Release
ATS Sourcing	Association Meetings	Job Fairs
Association Websites	Alumni Sourcing	Phone-A-Thon/Email Blasts

Challenge Statement Template

"How Might We..." Statements needs to include:
The What – what is the problem or challenge?
The Audience – who is the audience or key stakeholders – be specific?
The Change – what is the change you want to see?
Inspiring and Interesting – are you or the team excited and interested in solving the challenge?

Identify the problem/challenge:

_____

_____

What do you know about this already?

_____

_____

Why do you want to change this?

_____

_____

How Might We Statement:

How might we _____

_____

Review Challenge Statement and ask:

Is the solution in the statement?

Are you excited or interested in learning more?

Is it focus on your audience and focus on a specific timeframe?

If you answered **yes** to any of these, go back and update the Challenge Statement.

Final Challenge Statement:

_____

_____

_____

_____

Candidate Persona Template

Step One: Define Your Ideal Candidate

_____

_____

_____

_____

_____

_____

Step Two: Locate Ideal Candidate

_____

_____

_____

_____

_____

_____

Step Three: How to Engage Your Candidate

_____

_____

_____

_____

Step Four: Potential Sourcing Strategies to Pursue

_____

_____

_____

_____

_____

Job Posting Template

Goal of a Job Posting:	To provide potential new hires with an overview of the company, realistic job preview and the expectations and requirements needed to successfully succeed in the position.
Appearance:	The job posting is the first impression of your business. Ensure that it is professional and easy to read.
Employer Brand:	Brand the job posting with your logo and any additional branding (photos, employee testimonials, etc.)
Overview of the company:	Provide a brief overview of the company and this year's and future goals.
What is in it for me:	Potential new hires want to know what they will receive if they join the team. Provide information about compensation, benefits, culture, work environment, etc. Give them a realistic view of what you receive as an employee of the company. Employer Value Proposition can be included in this.
Realistic Job Preview:	A paragraph with a summary of the role plus bullet points on what this individual will be doing for the first year. Include any potential projects and how this role will benefit the company's goals.
Job Requirements:	In bullet format, provide any experience needed and hard skills. Do not include soft skills. For Affirmative Action employers: include must have experience/skills and preferred experience/skills in different sections.
Contact Information:	Provide how someone can apply to the position – website and/or contact information.
Legality Information:	If needed, provide any legality information at the end of the job posting. Speak to your attorney to ensure that you understand what is needed.
What Not to Do:	Large paragraphs of information will make the posting hard to read.
	Spelling and grammatical error are a big NO!
	Do not use different size fonts and lots of colors.
	Honesty is the best policy – do not exaggerate
	Do not add additional responsibilities or requirements if not included in the job description.

Onboarding Checklist

New Hire:

Start Date:

Item:	Owner:	Started:	Completed:	Initials:
Hire in System				
Welcome Email with Onboarding Details				
Welcome Call (Friday before start date)				
Request Workstation				
Request Office Set Up				
Request Phone (Cell/Landline)				
Request System Access				
Phone/Voicemail Set Up				
Printer Set Up				
Order Business Cards				
Select Mentor				
Email Introduction				
HR Paperwork				
Tour of Building				
Introduction to Team and Stakeholders				
Training Schedule				
Lunch with Team				
Schedule One on One Meetings				
Add to Team Meetings				
Review Company and Department Goals				
Review 30/60/90 Day Plan				

Mash Up Session Template

Goal is to take two completely different categories and put them together to generate creative or original ideas

1. Use your Challenge Statement for the mash up
2. Select one category that relates to the Challenge Statement and one category completely different (i.e. On-site Interviews and Dating)
3. In 2-3 minutes per category, write as many elements, experiences, items, etc. Goal is to get as many items on each list.

Category 1: (Interviewing)	Category 2: (Dating)

4. Mash Up – select one item from each category and create new ideas. Try to take items from each category that are completely different from each other and mash up. Take 3-5 minutes to come up with ideas.

Category 1:	Category 2:	Mash Up Idea

5. Review ideas and vote for the best idea.

Number of Ideas:	
Insights:	
Themes:	
#1 Idea per Votes	
#2 Idea per Votes	
#3 Idea per Votes	

Brainstorming Template

Brainstorming is a creative strategy for teams to generate ideas when they are trying to come up with quick potential solutions to a challenge.

1. Set Up:
   a. Use your Challenge Statement for the brainstorming session
   b. Space with no distractions (conference room, off site meeting space, etc.)
   c. Designated Timekeeper and Facilitator
   d. Materials: post-it notes, markers, and a blank wall for recording ideas
   e. Decide on Individual or Group Brainstorming (5-6 people in group)
   f. Decide on number of minutes to brainstorm (10-15 minutes).
2. Rules:
   a. Defer judgement
   b. Generate as many ideas as possible – the good, the bad, and the ugly.
   c. Stay focused on the challenge statement
   d. After brainstorming, the group will bucket ideas by themes, discuss ideas and vote for their favorite(s).

Ideas:

# of Ideas:			

Themes:

Votes:

#1 Idea:	
#2 Idea:	
#3 Idea:	
#4 Idea:	
#5 Idea:	

Selected Idea:	

Recruiter Score Card Template

Personal Goals:	
Team Goals:	

Class Base Hiring:	Monthly	ATS Audit	Monthly
# of Candidates		Statuses	
# of Tests		Evaluations	
Applicant to Hire Ratio		Interviewer Listed	
Test to Hire Ratio		Job Posting Details	
Class Base Hiring:		High Fives:	
Goal:			
Actual:			
% of Fill:			
Candidate Survey			
New Hire Survey			
Hiring Manager Survey			
HM to Hire Ratio			
Offer to Hire Ratio			
# of HM Interviews			
# of Offers			
HM to Offer Ratio			
Internal One Off Reqs:		Survey Results:	Hiring Managers
Average Date to Fill:			
Applicant to Hire Ratio			
PI to Hire Ratio			
HM to Offer Ratio			
HM to Hire Ratio			
Offer to Hire Ratio			
External One Off Reqs:		Survey Results:	Candidates
Average Date to Fill:			
Applicant to Hire Ratio			
PI to Hire Ratio			
HM to Offer Ratio			
HM to Hire Ratio			
Offer to Hire Ratio			
Project Work:		Survey Results:	New Hires
Project 1:			
Project 2:			

Observation Template

Planning: Before observation, you must know **who** to observe, **where** to observe and **what** to look for.

Who	Where	What

Observation Notes:

Who:	
Where:	
Observations:	
Insights:	

Who:	
Where:	
Observations:	
Insights:	

Who:	
Where:	
Observations:	
Insights:	

Interviewing Template

Based on your Challenge Statement, decide who you want to interview and select up to 10 questions that will help you learn about the challenge and audience.

Interviewing Questions:

1.	
2.	
3.	
4.	
5.	
6.	
7.	
8.	
9.	
10.	

Name of Interviewee:	
Date:	
Where:	
Insights from Interview	
Name of Interviewee:	
Date:	
Where:	
Insights from Interview	
Name of Interviewee:	
Date:	
Where:	
Insights from Interview	

Overall Insights:	
Overall Themes:	
Quotes:	
Stories:	

SOURCES

1. A Perspective on Talent Acquisition and Design Thinking

1. "Press: The Conference Board," 2 January 2020. [Online]. Available: https://www.conference-board.org/press/c-suite-survey-2020. [Accessed 15 April 2020].
2. "About: Press: iHire," iHire, 2 December 2019. [Online]. Available: https://www.ihire.com/about/press/ihire-survey-small-businesses-struggle-to-attract-qualified-talent. [Accessed 15 April 2020].
3. "Press: The Conference Board," 2 January 2020. [Online]. Available: https://www.conference-board.org/press/c-suite-survey-2020. [Accessed 15 April 2020].
4. "Insights: Duke Fuqua," Duke Fuqua School of Business, 17 April 2019. [Online]. Available: https://www.fuqua.duke.edu/duke-fuqua-insights/cfo-survey-q1-2019. [Accessed 15 April 2020].
5. R. R. a. Q. Forget, "News: Politico," Politico, 9 April 2020. [Online]. Available: https://www.politico.com/news/2020/04/09/coronavirus-unemployment-claims-numbers-176794. [Accessed 15 April 2020].
6. N. N. a. F. W. Ranjay Gulati, "Recession: HBR," Harvard Business Review, March 2010. [Online]. Available: https://hbr.org/2010/03/roaring-out-of-recession. [Accessed 16 April 2020].
7. N. N. a. F. W. Ranjay Gulati, "Recession: HBR," Harvard Business Review, March 2010. [Online]. Available: https://hbr.org/2010/03/roaring-out-of-recession. [Accessed 16 April 2020].
8. "Case Study: IDEO," IDEO, 2018. [Online]. Available: https://www.ideo.com/case-study/a-new-employment-venture-to-increase-customer-engagement-and-financial-security. [Accessed 17 April 2020].

2. Design Thinking

1. "Case Study: IDEO," IDEO, 2018. [Online]. Available: https://www.ideo.com/case-study/reimagining-everyday-travel-for-america-and-beyond . [Accessed 20 April 2020].
2. T. Brown, "Design Thinking: IDEO," IDEO, [Online]. Available: https://designthinking.ideo.com/. [Accessed 20 April 2020].
3. "Products: IDEO U," IDEO U, [Online]. Available: https://www.ideou.com/products/from-ideas-to-action. [Accessed 20 April 2020].
4. "Main Page: IDEO U," IDEO U, [Online]. Available: https://www.ideou.com/.
5. "Products: IDEO U," IDEO U, [Online]. Available: https://www.ideou.com/products/from-ideas-to-action. [Accessed 20 April 2020].
6. "Products: IDEO U," IDEO U, [Online]. Available: https://www.ideou.com/products/from-ideas-to-action. [Accessed 20 April 2020].

3. Talent Acquisition Strategy With Related Challenge Statement

1. K. Tatley, "Employer: Zippia," Zippia, [Online]. Available: https://www.zippia.com/employer/steve-jobs-top-hiring-tip-hire-the-best. [Accessed 1 May 2020].

4. Recruitment Marketing Strategies With Storyboards

1. "Case Study: Phenom People," 2019. [Online]. Available: https://go.phenompeople.com/rs/392-IYN-961/images/PhenomPeople_CaseStudy_RentPath.pdf. [Accessed 5 May 2020].
2. "Research: The Talent Board," [Online]. Available: https://www.thetalentboard.org/benchmark-research/cande-research-reports/. [Accessed 7 May 2020].

5. Selection Process With Mash-Up Technique

1. "Pages: IDEO U," [Online]. Available: https://www.ideou.com/pages/ideation-method-mash-up. [Accessed 5 May 2020].

6. Talent Acquisition Technology And Brainstorming

1. "Main Page: pymetrics," pymetrics, [Online]. Available: https://www.pymetrics.ai/. [Accessed 10 May 2020].
2. P. Frida Polli, Interviewee, *CEO and Founder of pymetrics*. [Interview]. 27 May 2020.
3. P. Frida Polli, Interviewee, *CEO and Founder of pymetrics*. [Interview]. 27 May 2020.
4. P. Frida Polli, Interviewee, *CEO and Founder of pymetrics*. [Interview]. 27 May 2020.
5. "Pages: IDEO U," IDEO U, [Online]. Available: https://www.ideou.com/pages/brainstorming. [Accessed 10 May 2020].
6. "Pages: IDEO U," IDEO U, [Online]. Available: https://www.ideou.com/pages/brainstorming. [Accessed 10 May 2020].

7. People Experience And Empathy

1. "Research: The Talent Board," [Online]. Available: https://www.thetalentboard.org/benchmark-research/cande-research-reports/. [Accessed 7 May 2020].
2. "Research: The Talent Board," [Online]. Available: https://www.thetalentboard.org/benchmark-research/cande-research-reports/. [Accessed 7 May 2020].
3. "Research: The Talent Board," [Online]. Available: https://www.thetalentboard.org/benchmark-research/cande-research-reports/. [Accessed 7 May 2020].
4. "Dictionary: Merriam Webster," Merriam Webster, [Online]. Available: https://www.merriam-webster.com/dictionary/empathy. [Accessed 10 May 2020].
5. "Products: IDEO U," IDEO U, [Online]. Available: https://www.ideou.com/products/insights-for-innovation.

8. Communication for the Extremes

1. "Case Studies: The Talentboard," The Talentboard, [Online]. Available: https://www.thetalentboard.org/case-studies/point-click-care/. [Accessed 10 May 2020].

10. Retention of Top Performers using Observation and Interviewing

1. P. McCord, "Human Resource Management: HBR," January 2014. [Online]. Available: https://hbr.org/2014/01/how-netflix-reinvented-hr. [Accessed 12 May 2020].
2. J. Murphy, "Blog: SnackNation," 7 May 2020. [Online]. Available: https://snacknation.com/blog/how-to-retain-employees/. [Accessed 10 May 2020].

11. Next Steps And Iteration

1. "AZ Quotes," AZ Quotes, [Online]. Available: https://www.azquotes.com/author/2257-Nolan_Bushnell. [Accessed 10 May 2020].

www.ingramcontent.com/pod-product-compliance
Lightning Source LLC
Chambersburg PA
CBHW071425210326
41597CB00020B/3656